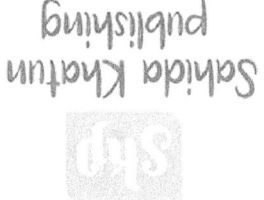

Sahida Khatun
publishing

Have any question ? Let us know
sahidakhatunpublishing@gmail.com

https://www.linkedin.com/in/sahida-khatun-publishing-9331003203

After you buy this book
please give us an honest feedback

★ ★ ★ ★ ★

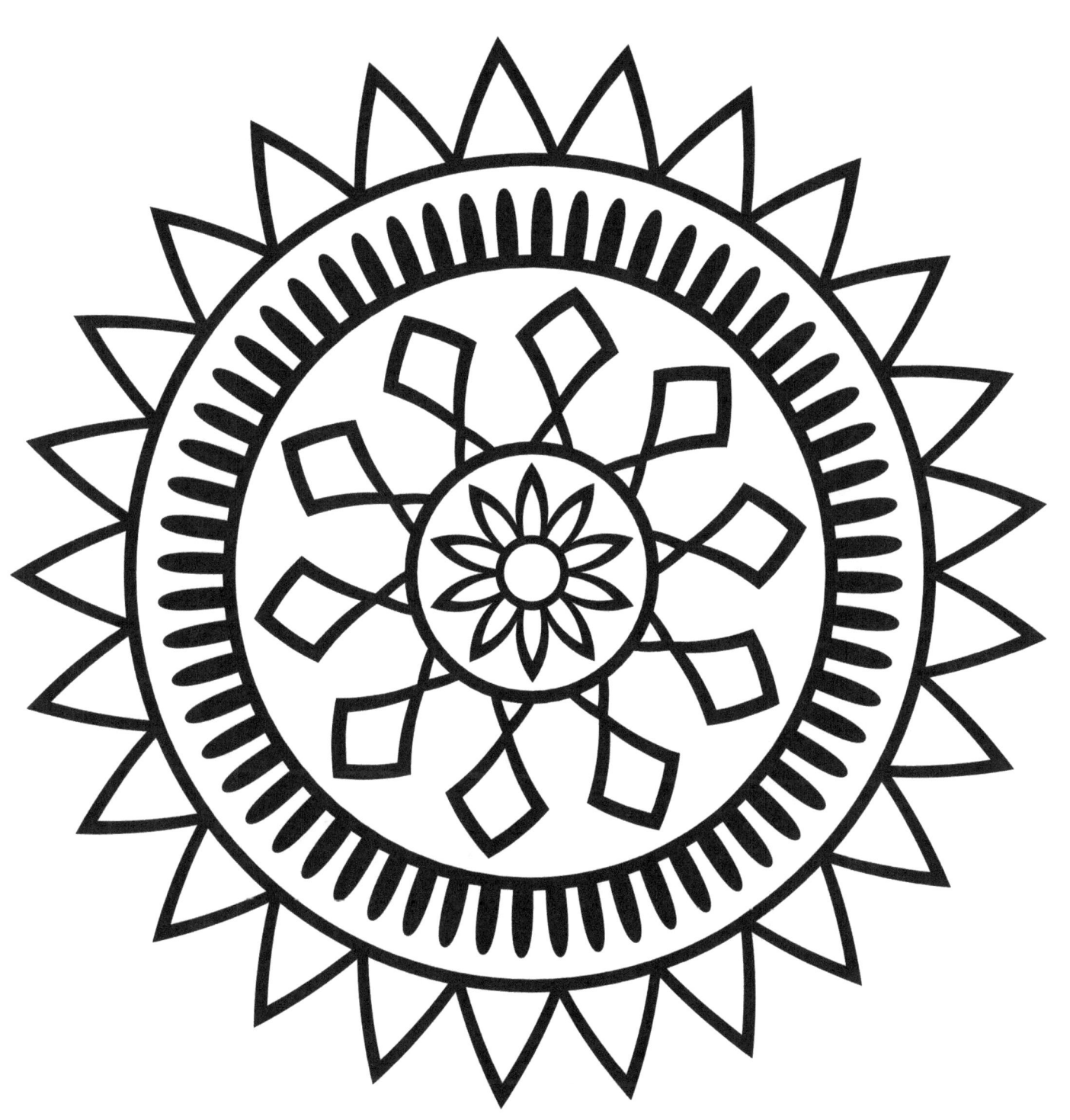

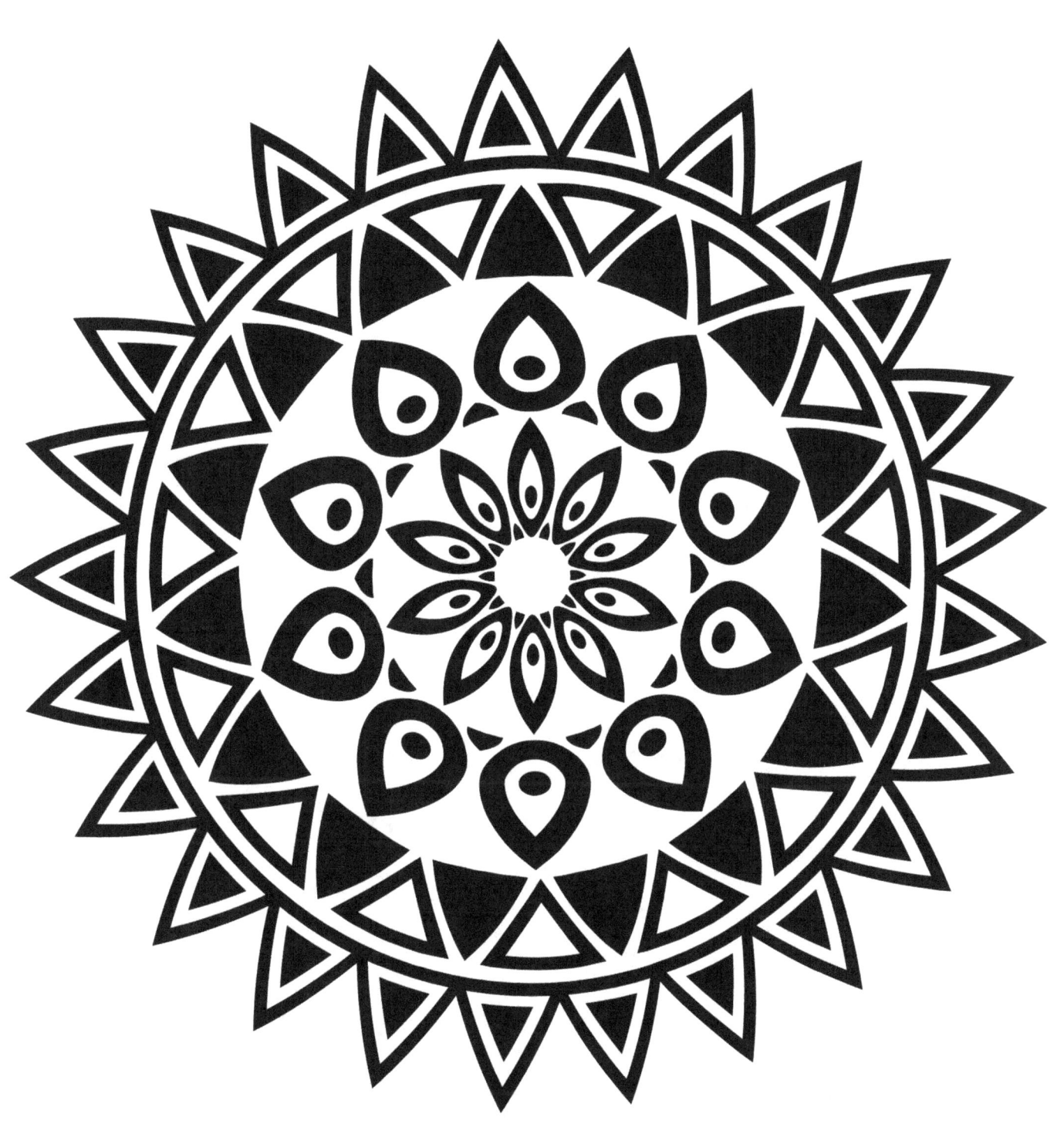

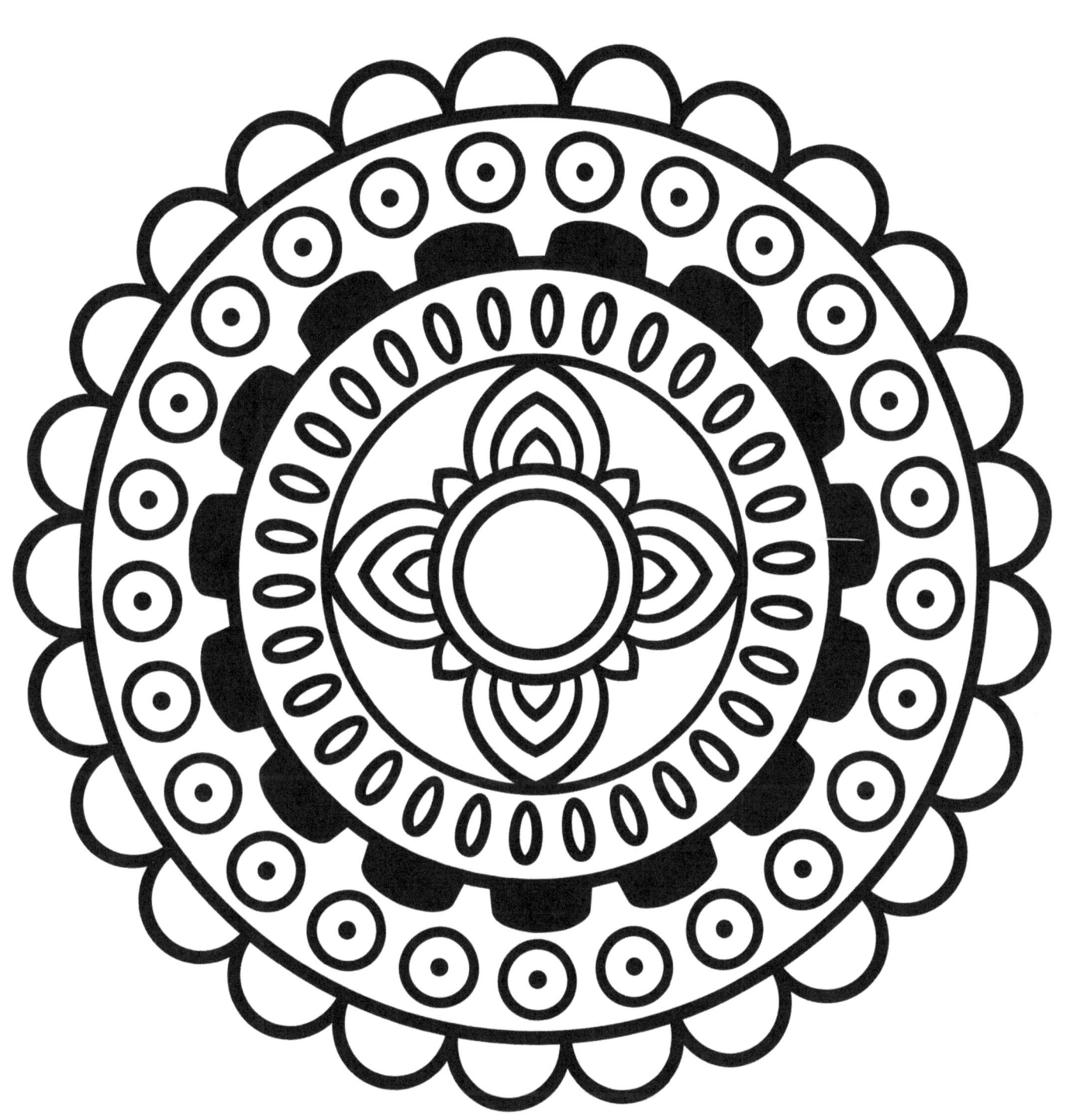

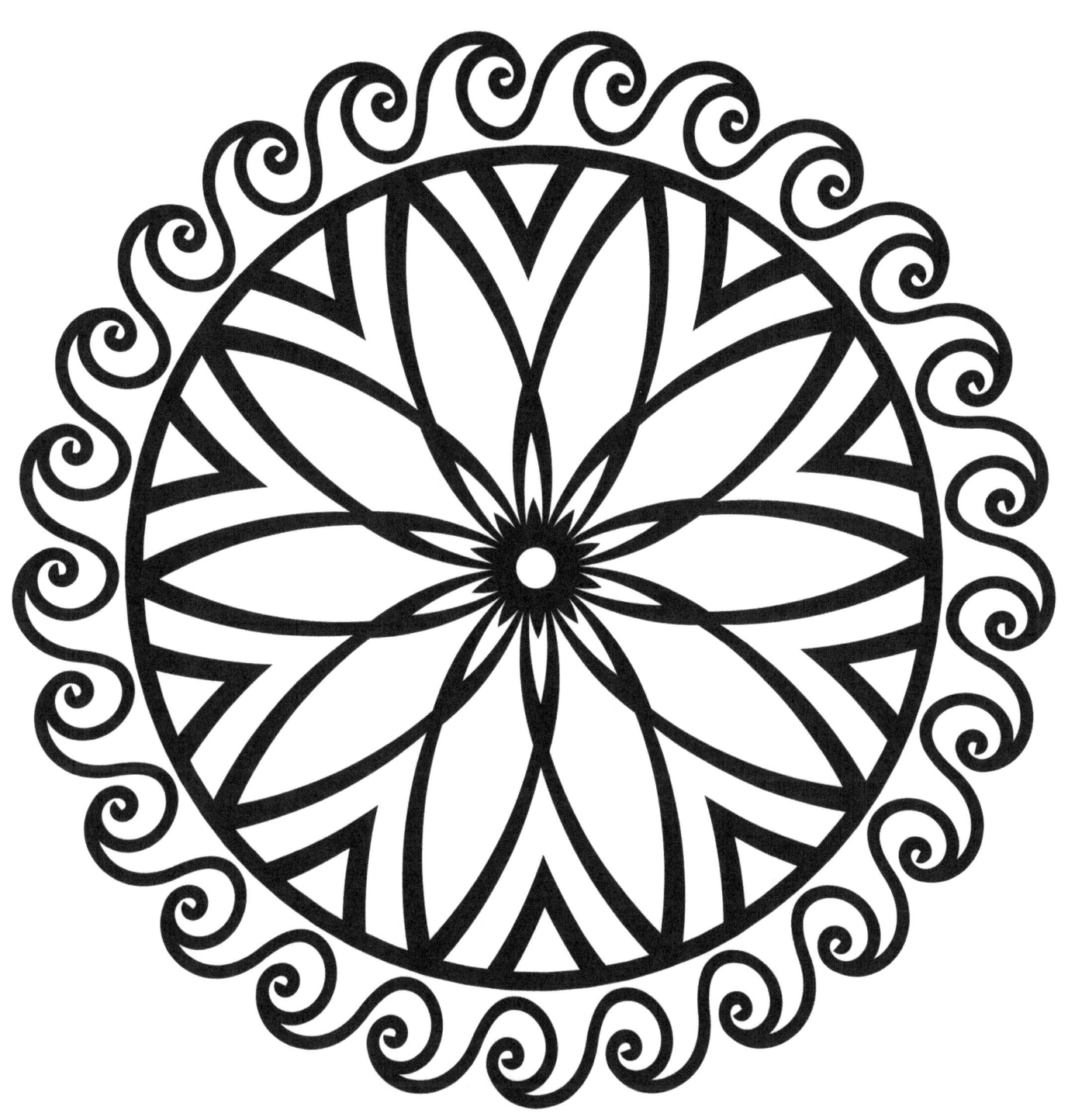

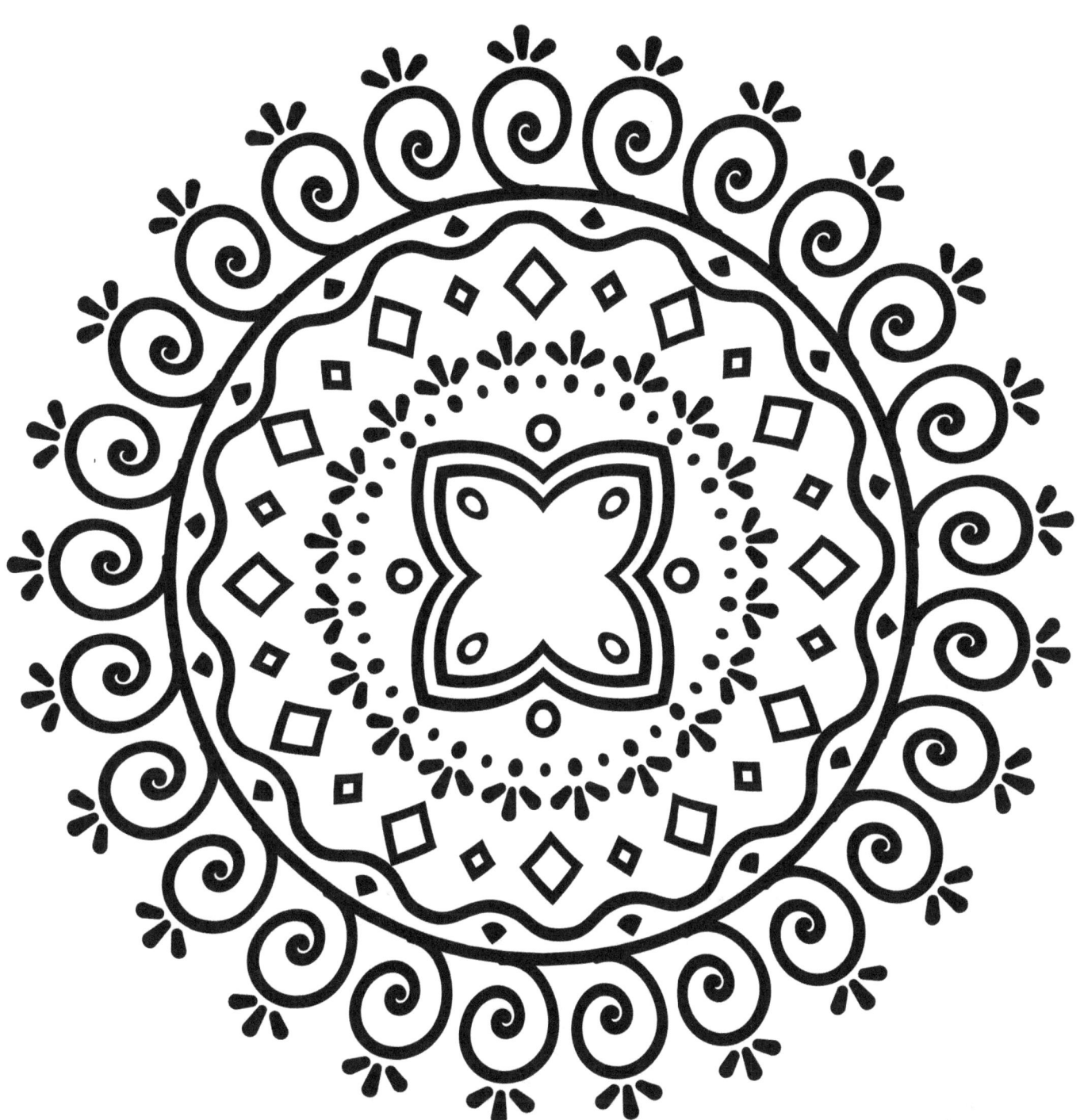

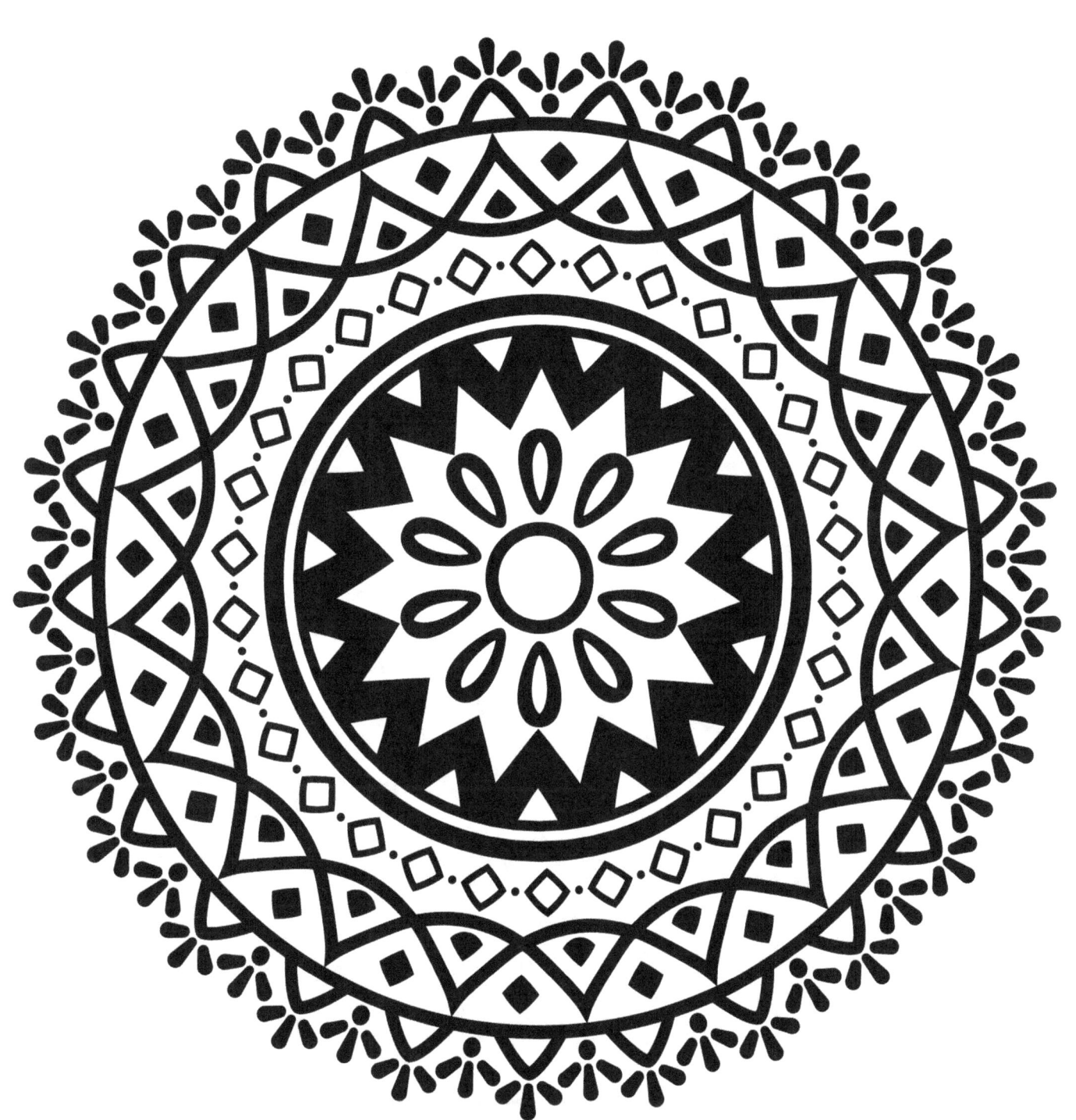

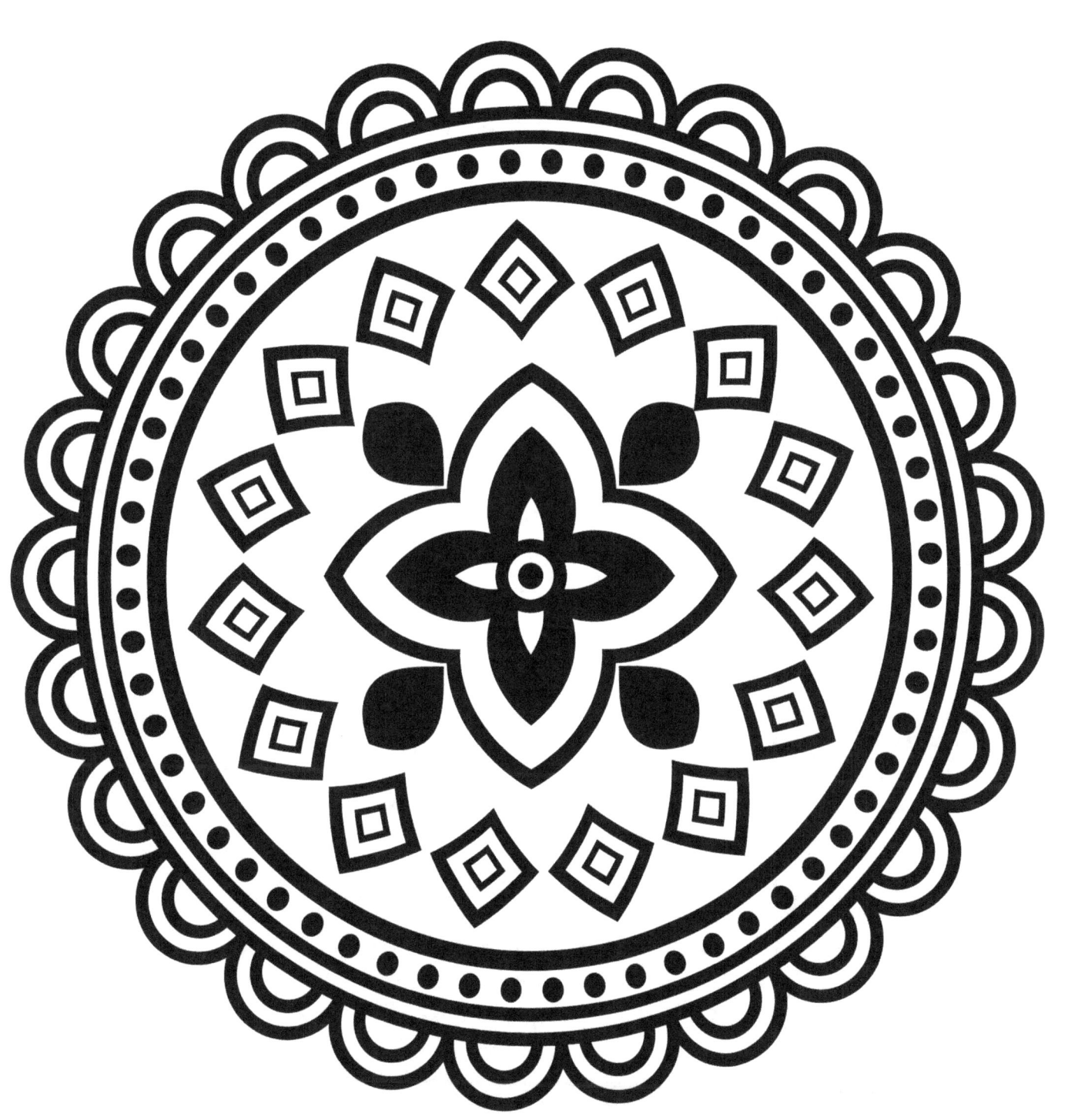

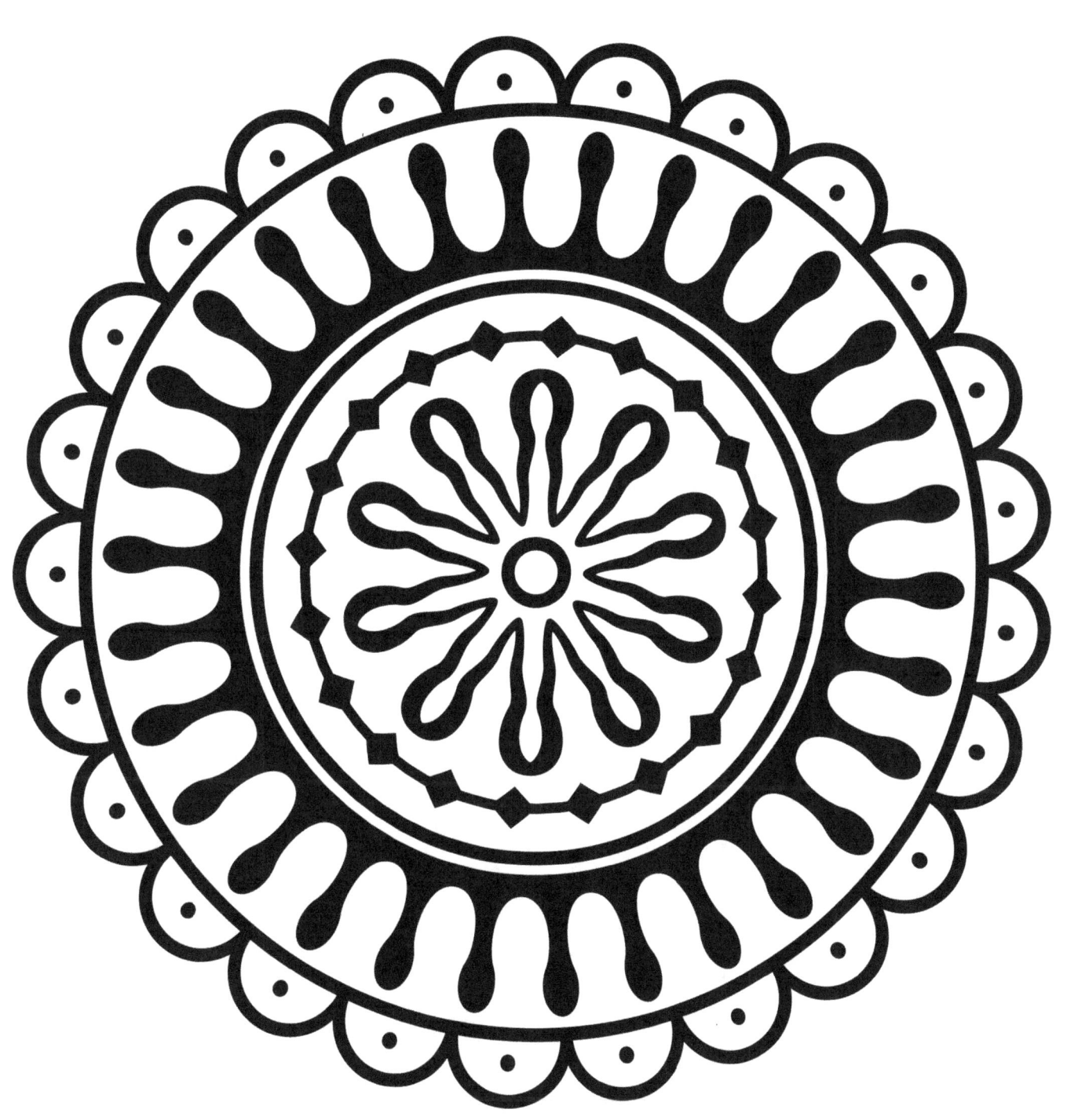

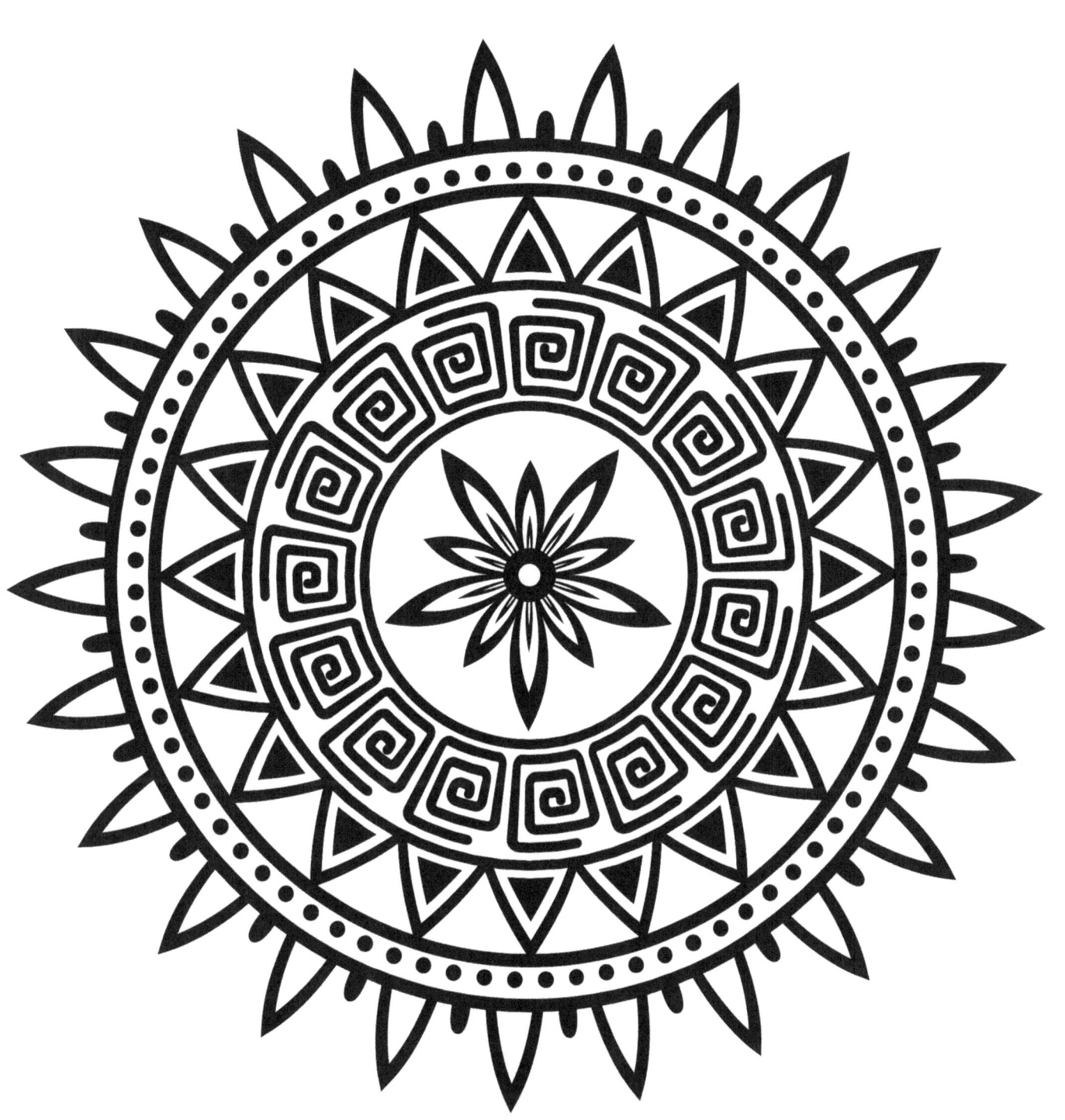

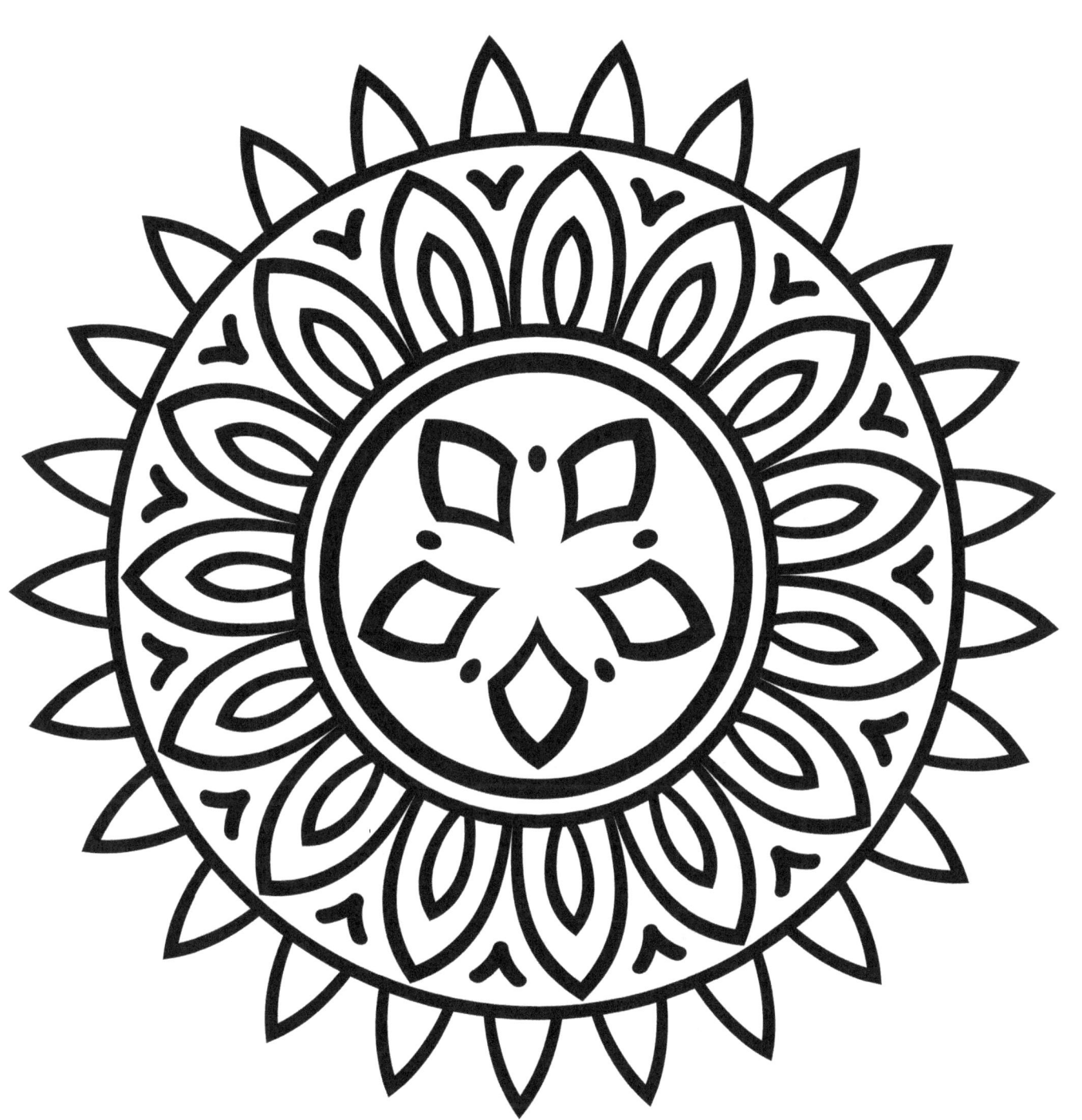

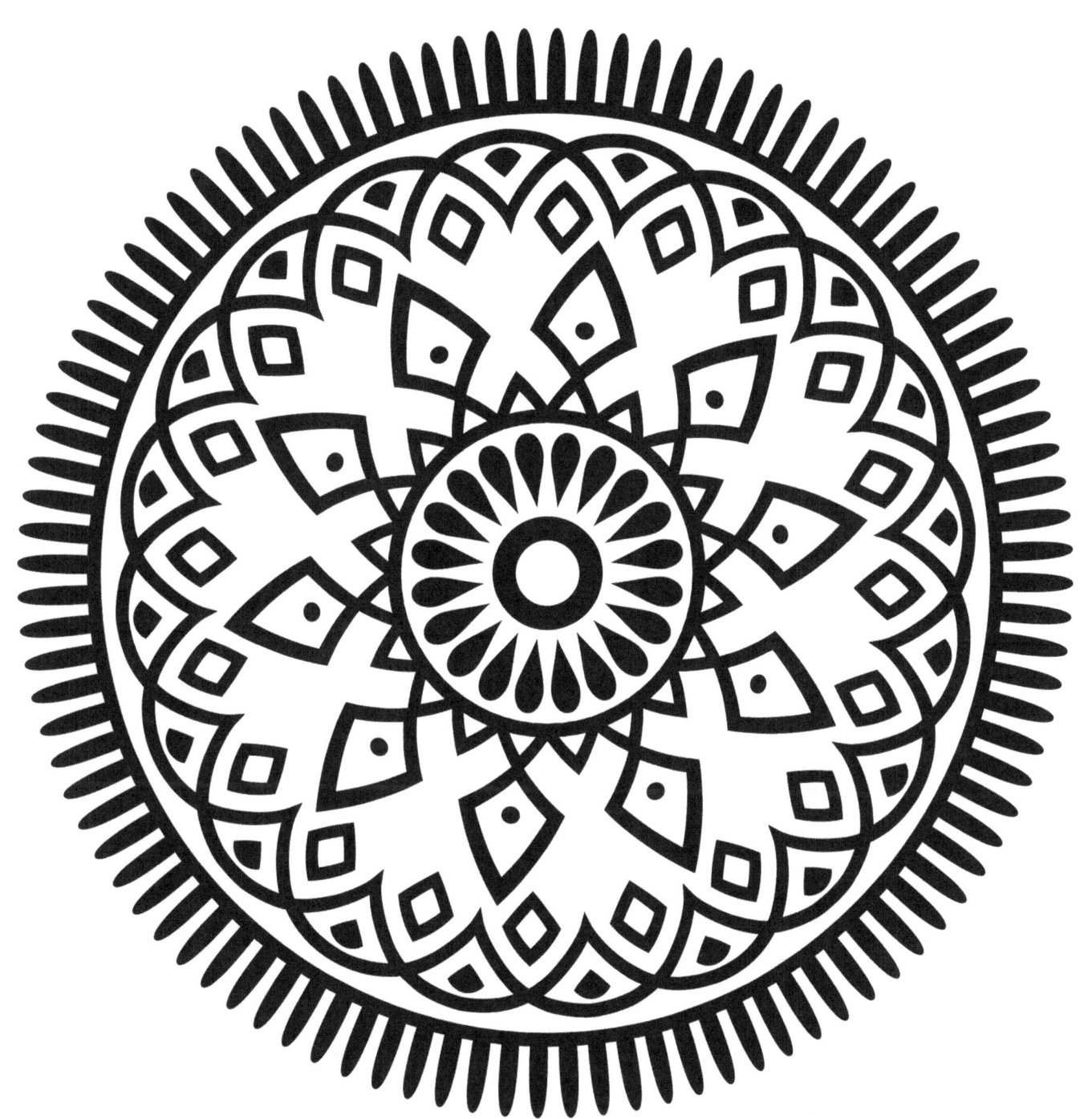

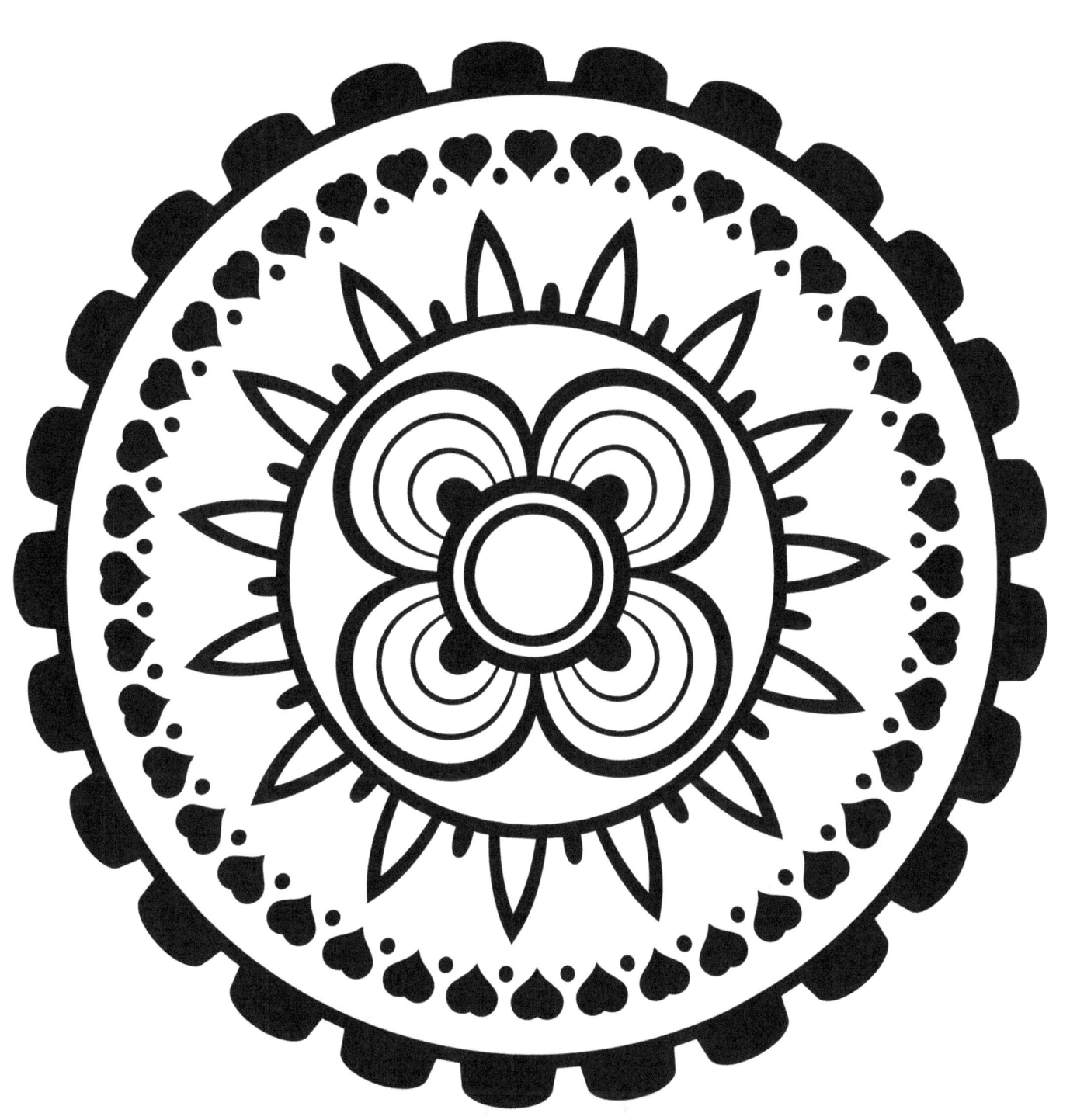

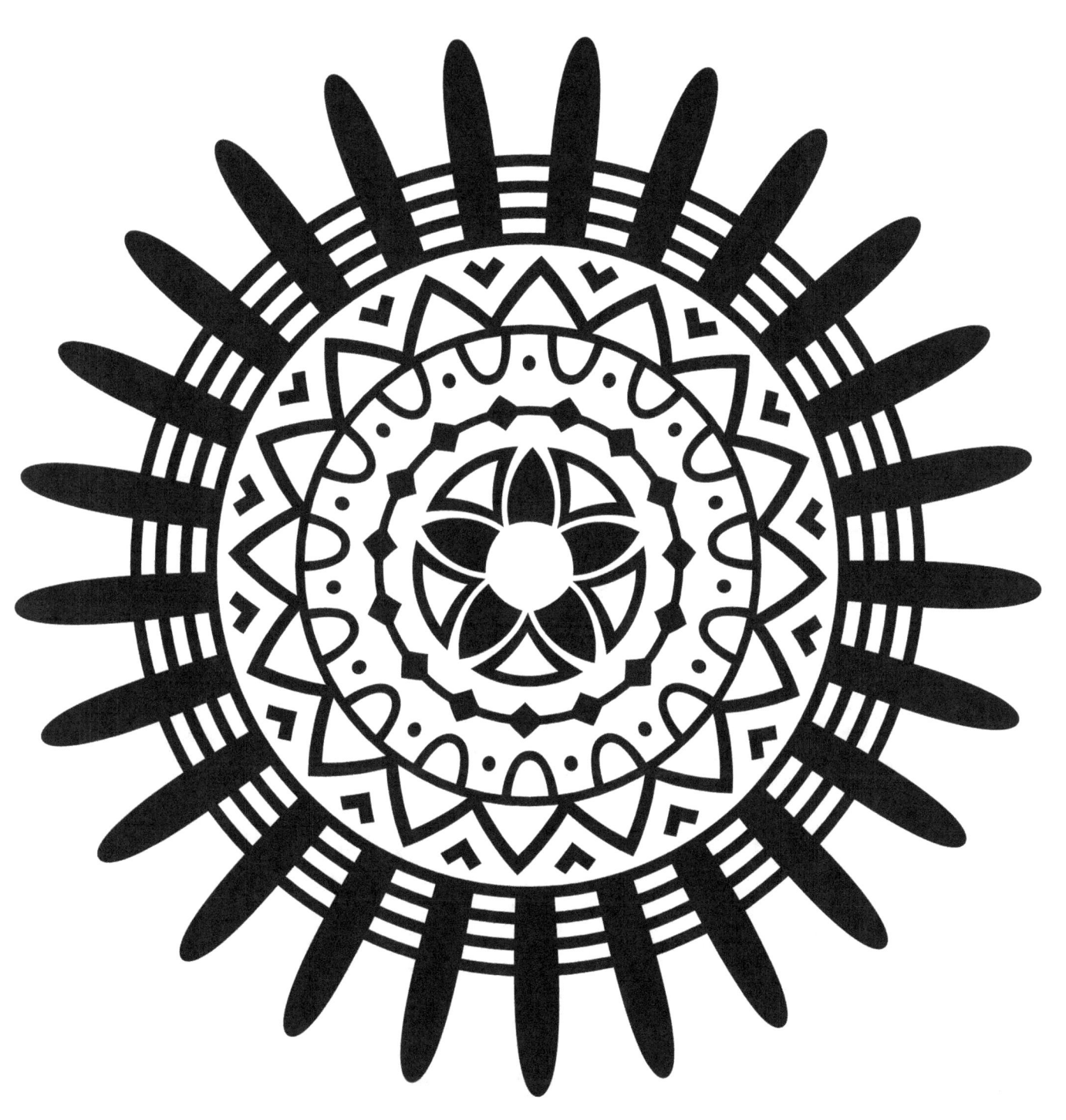

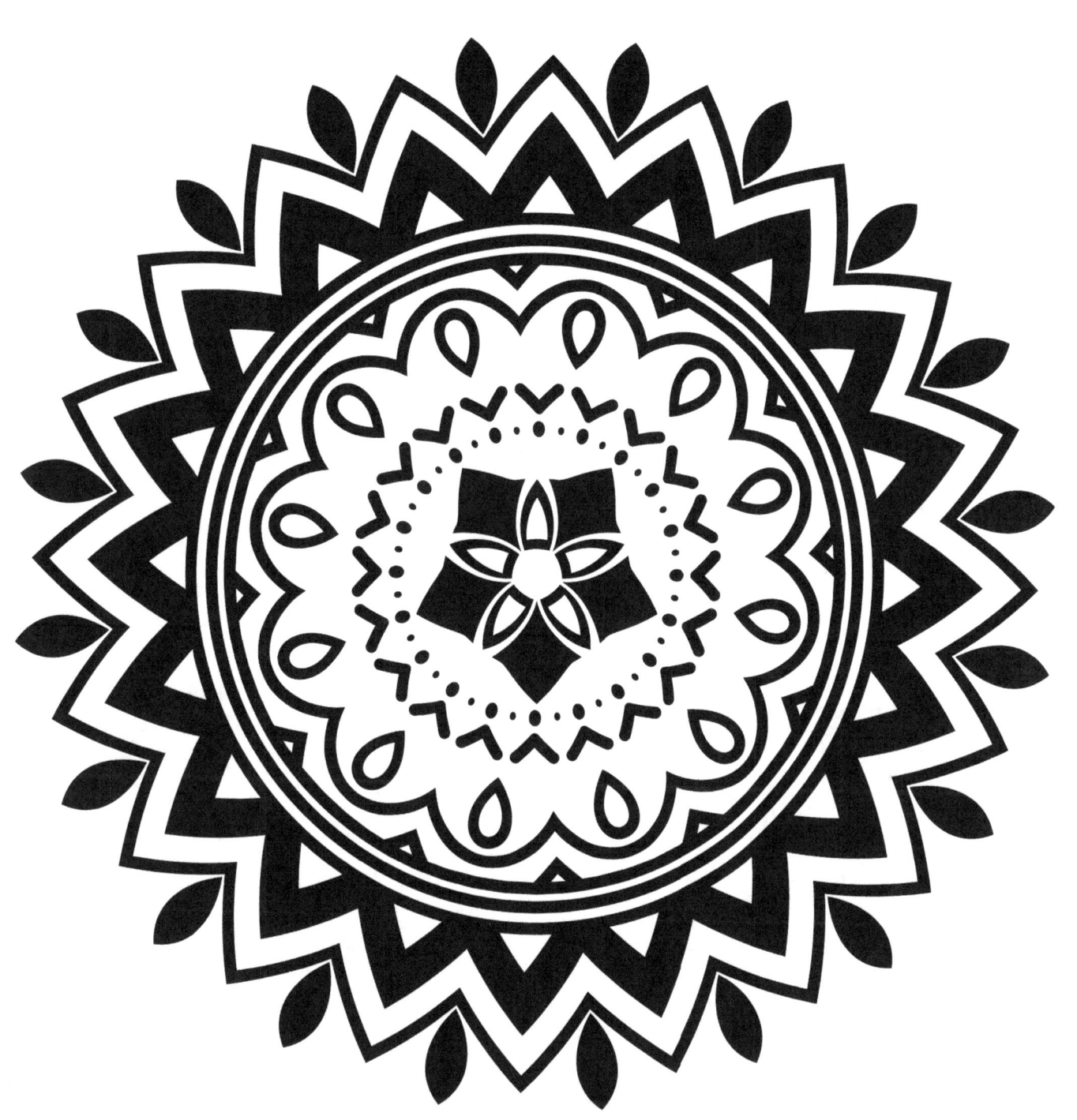

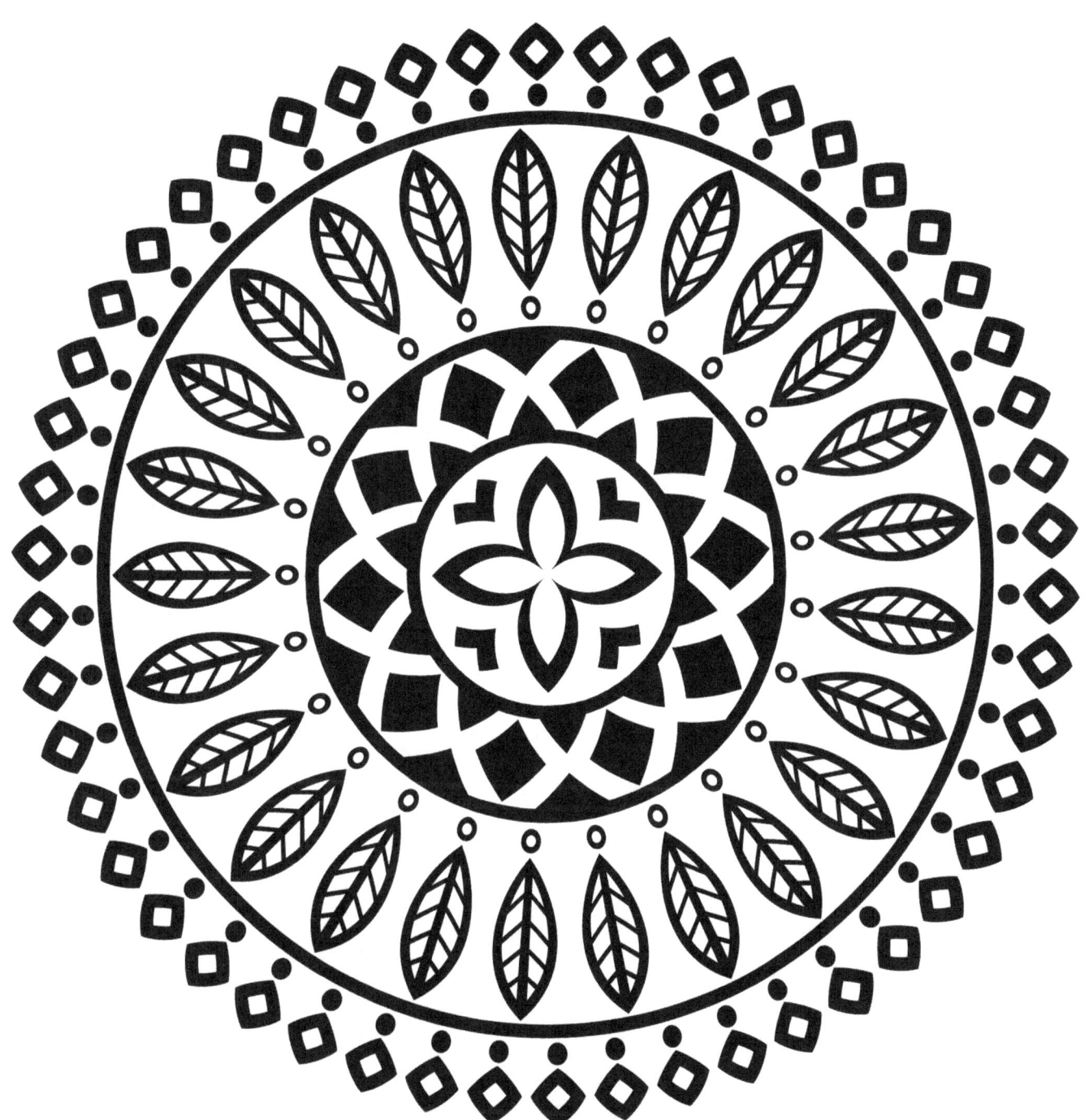

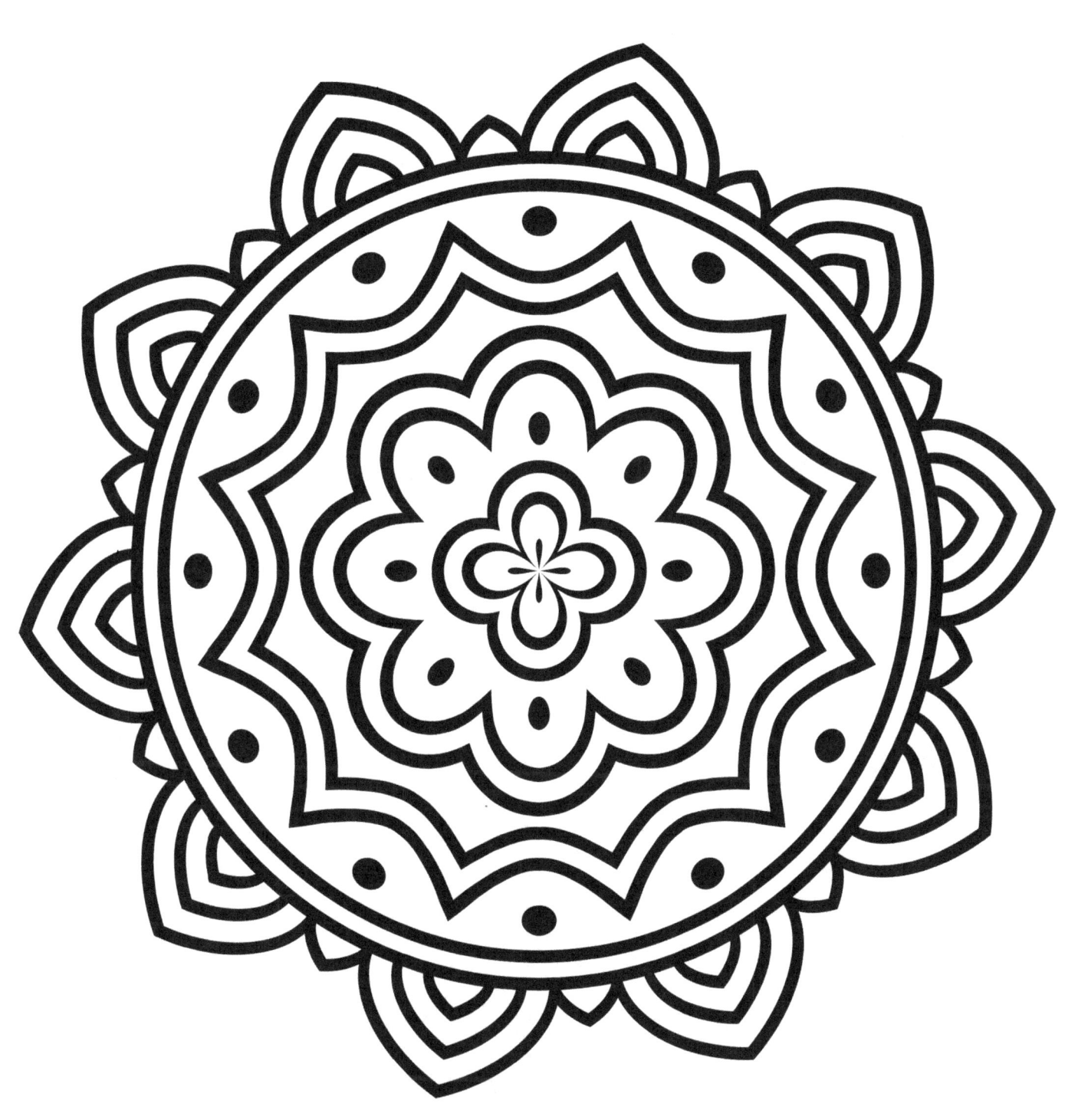

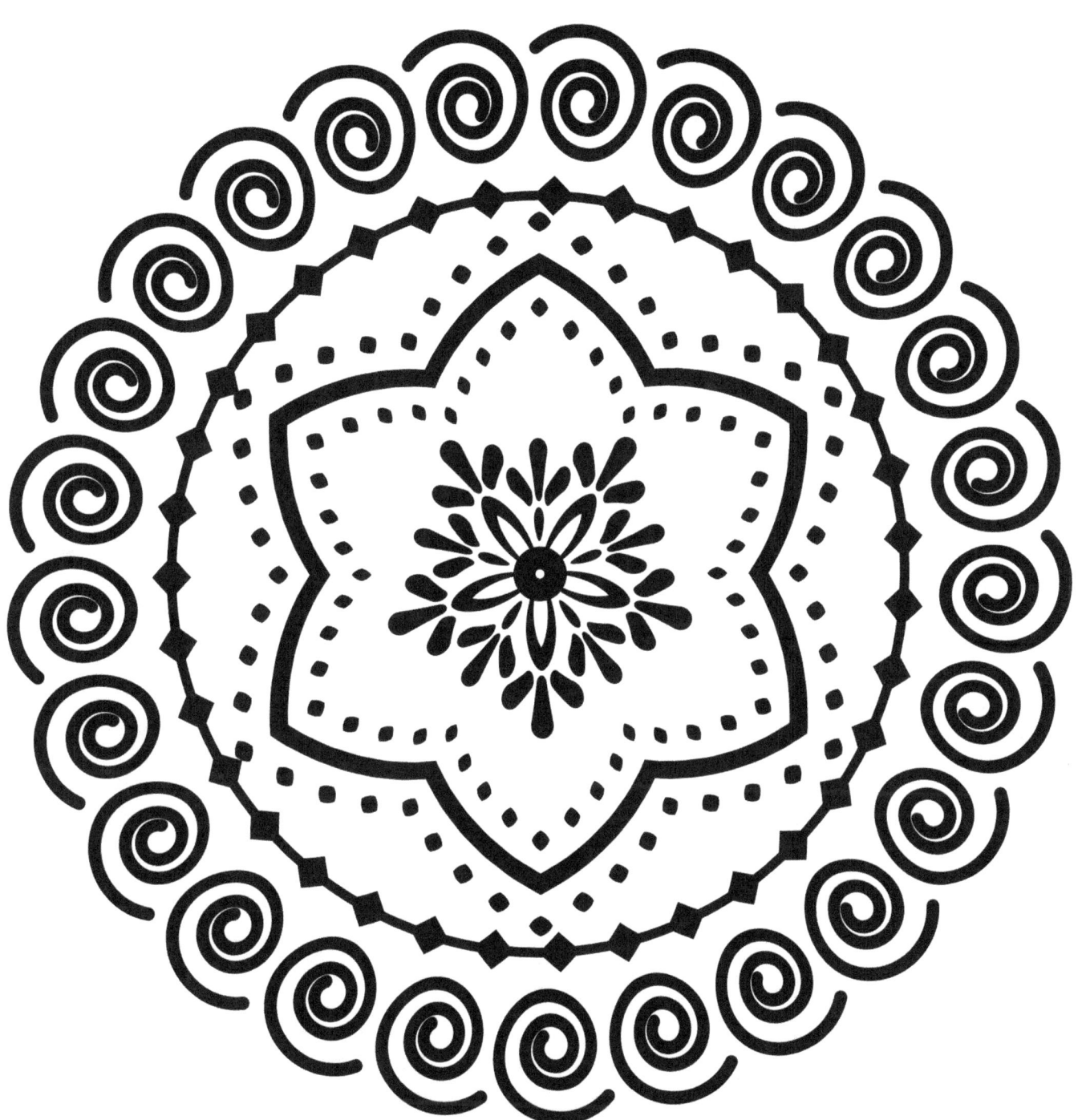

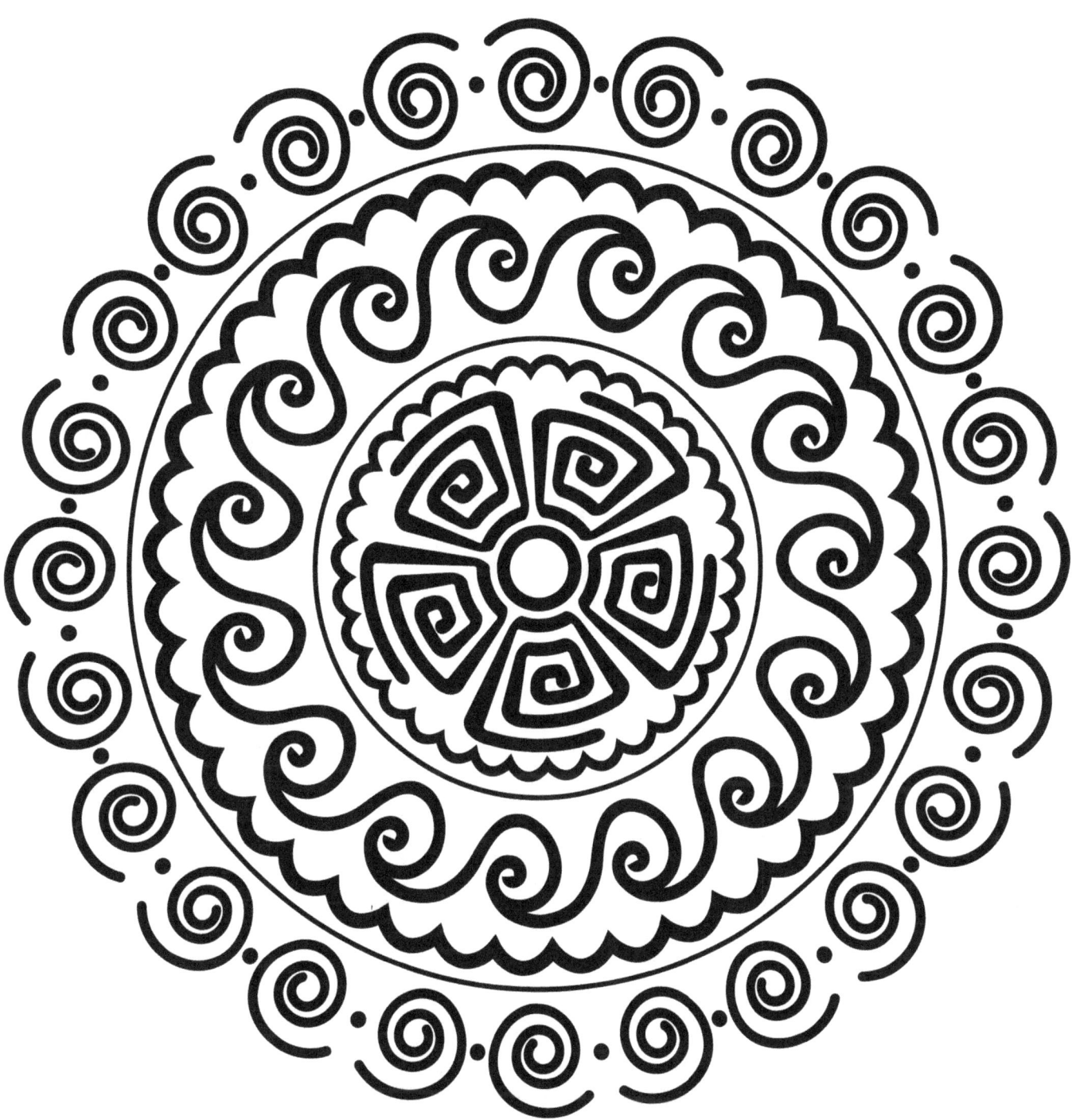

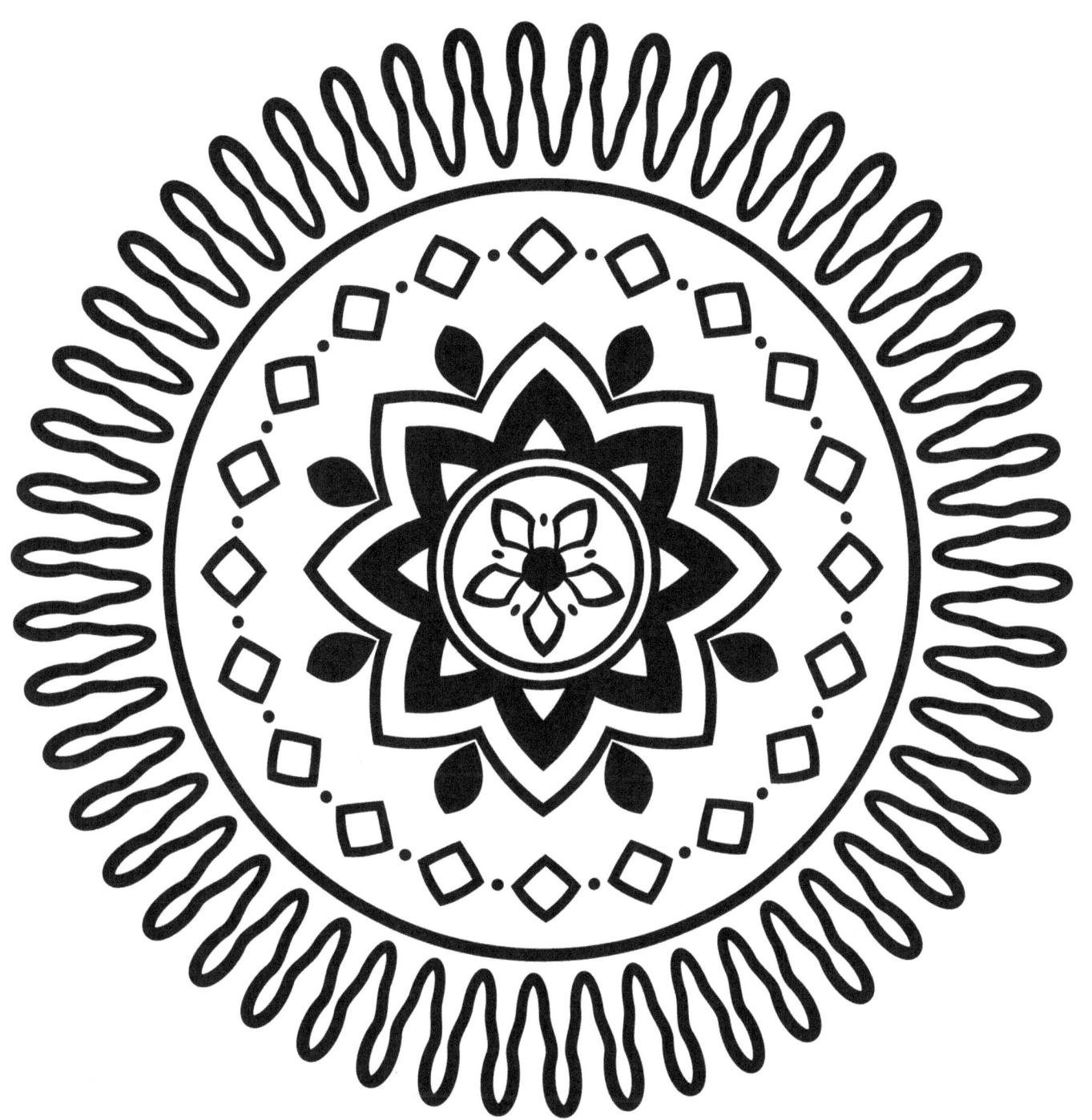

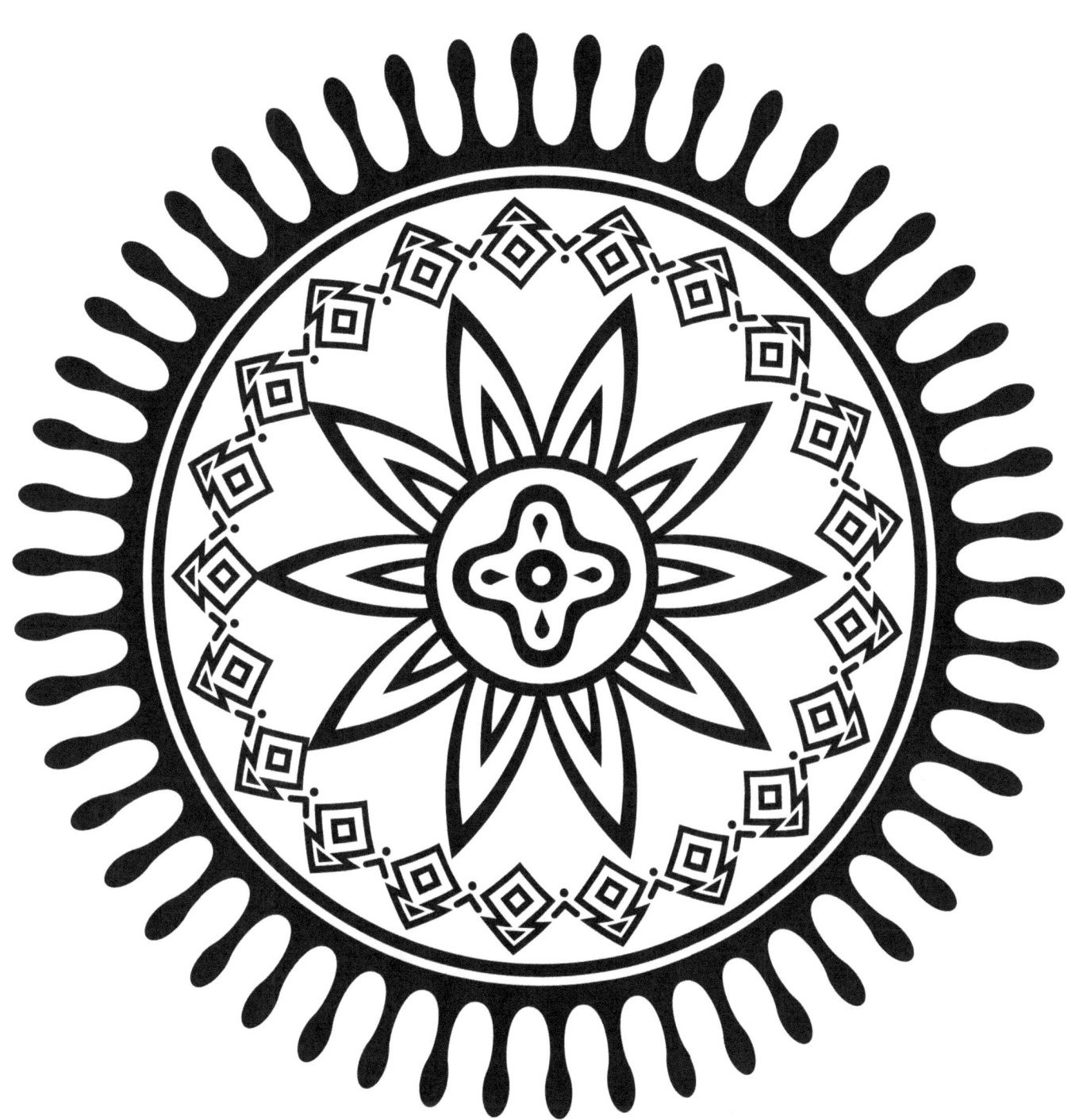

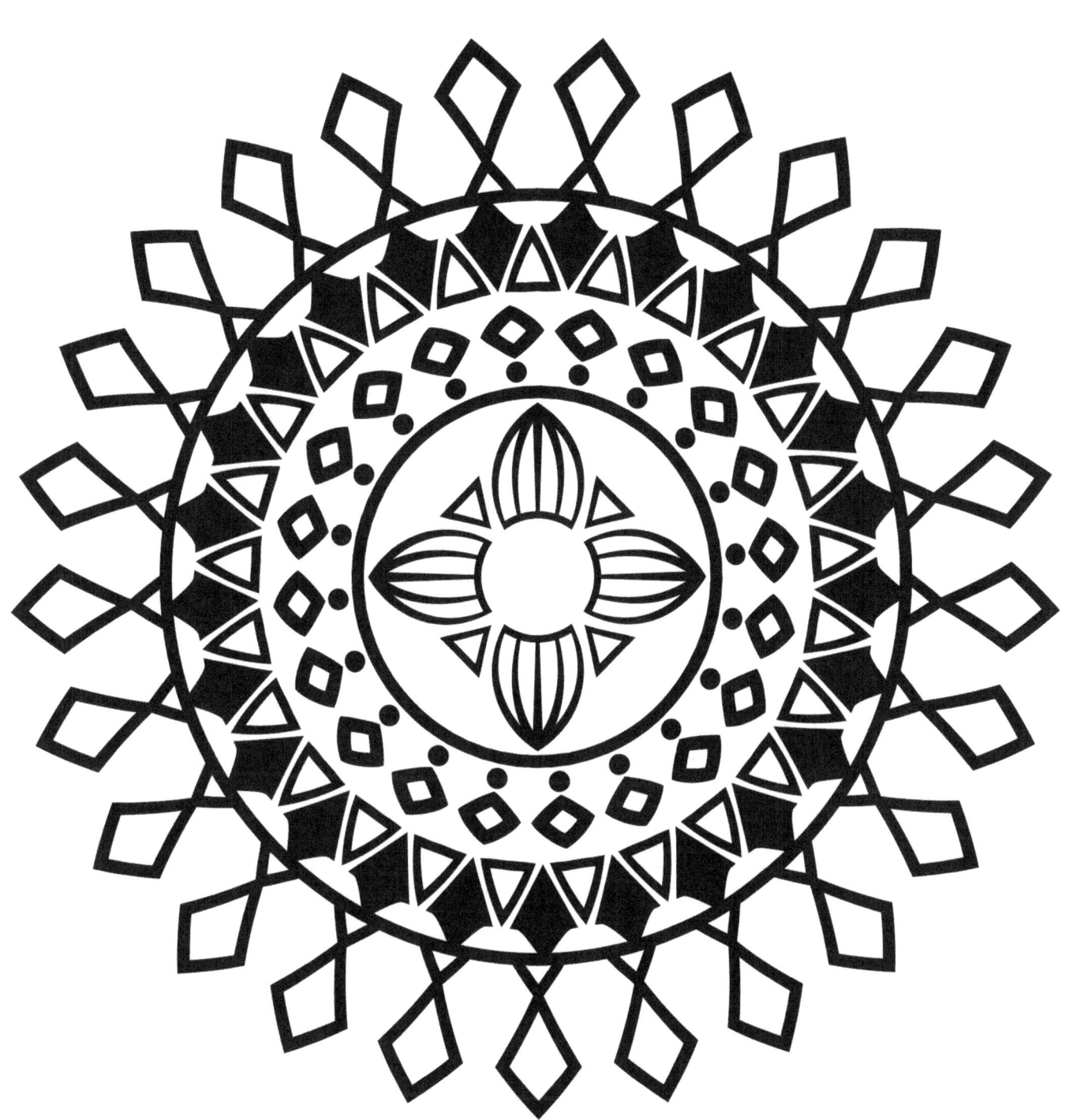

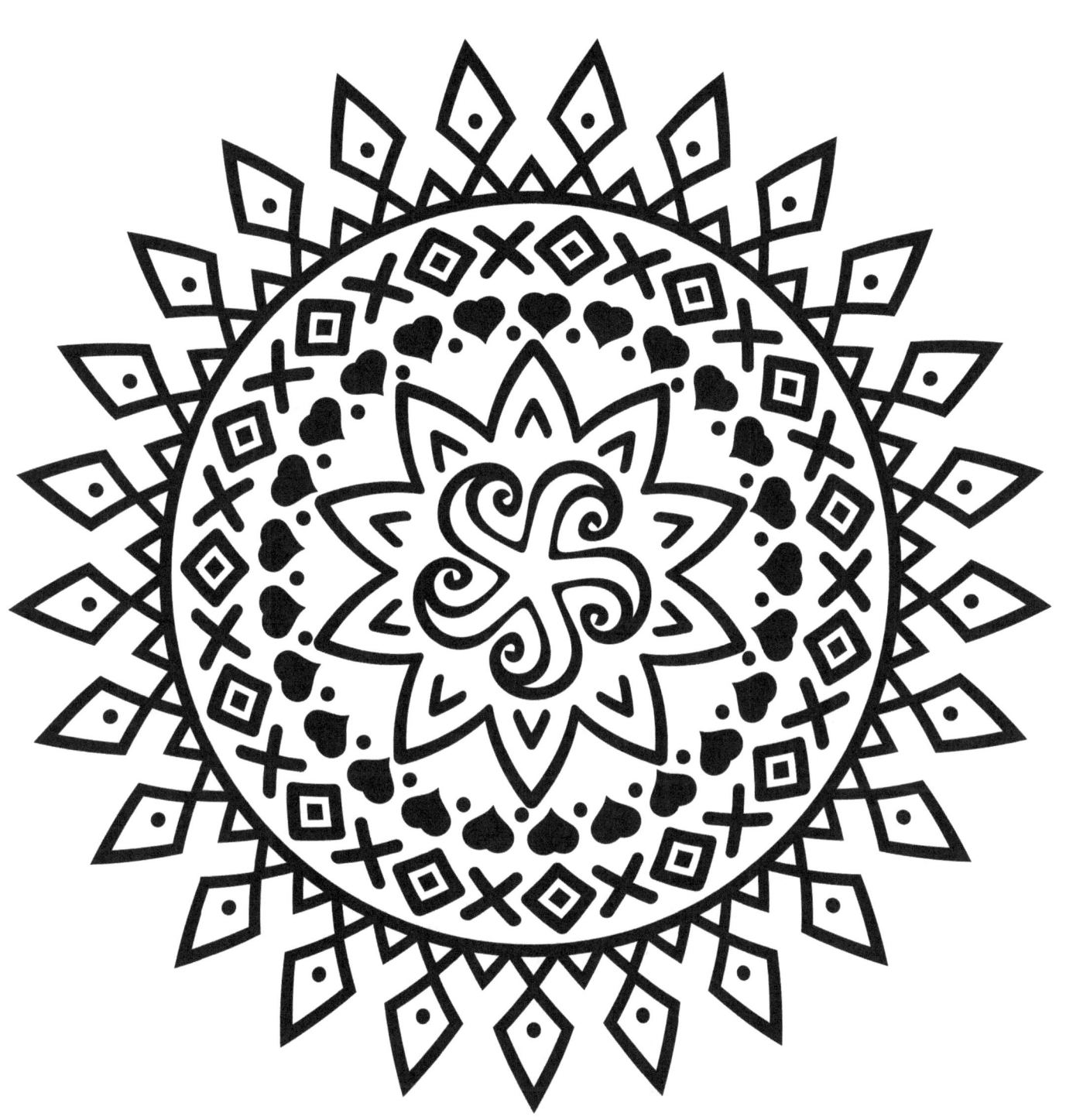

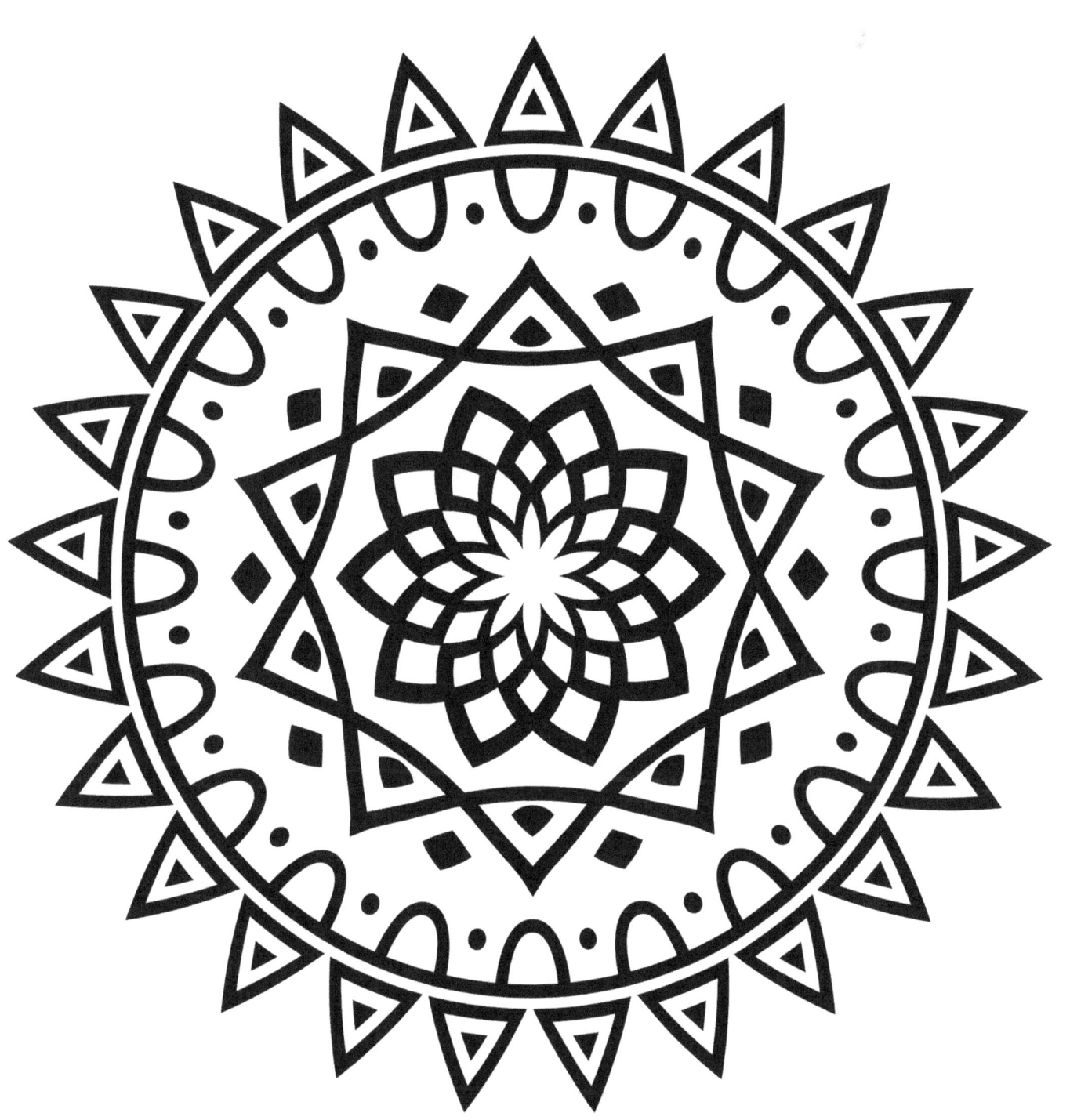

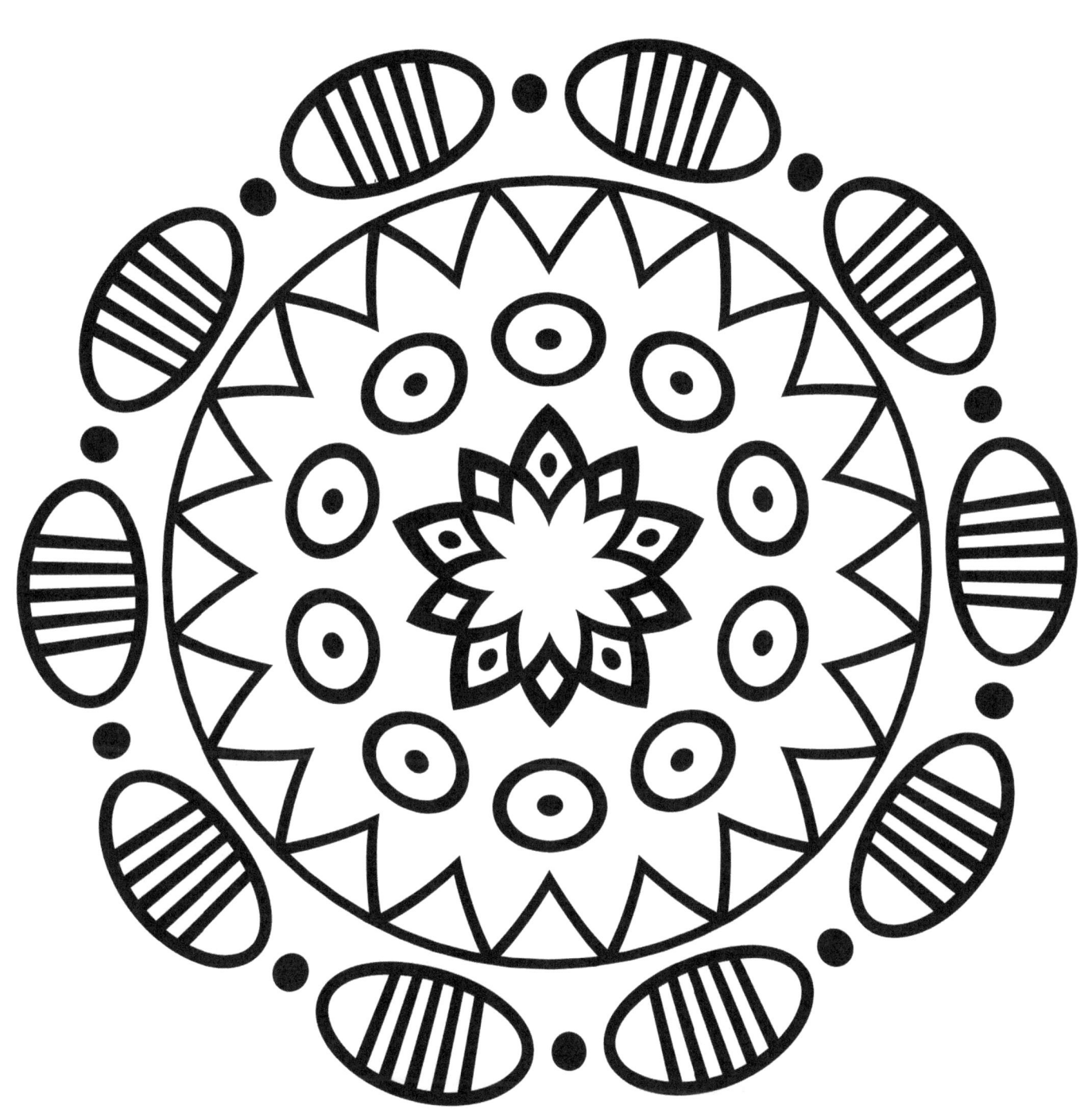

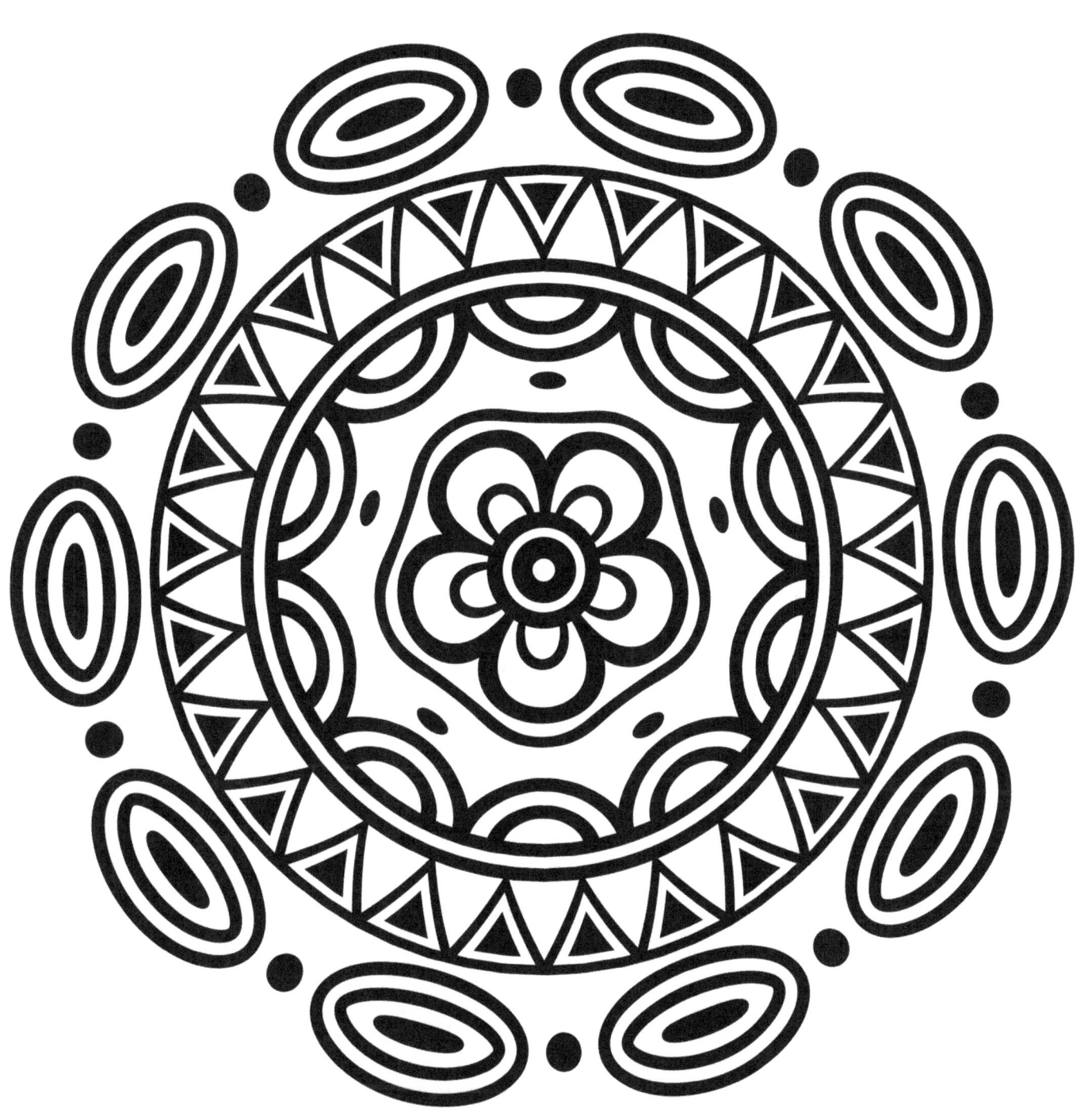

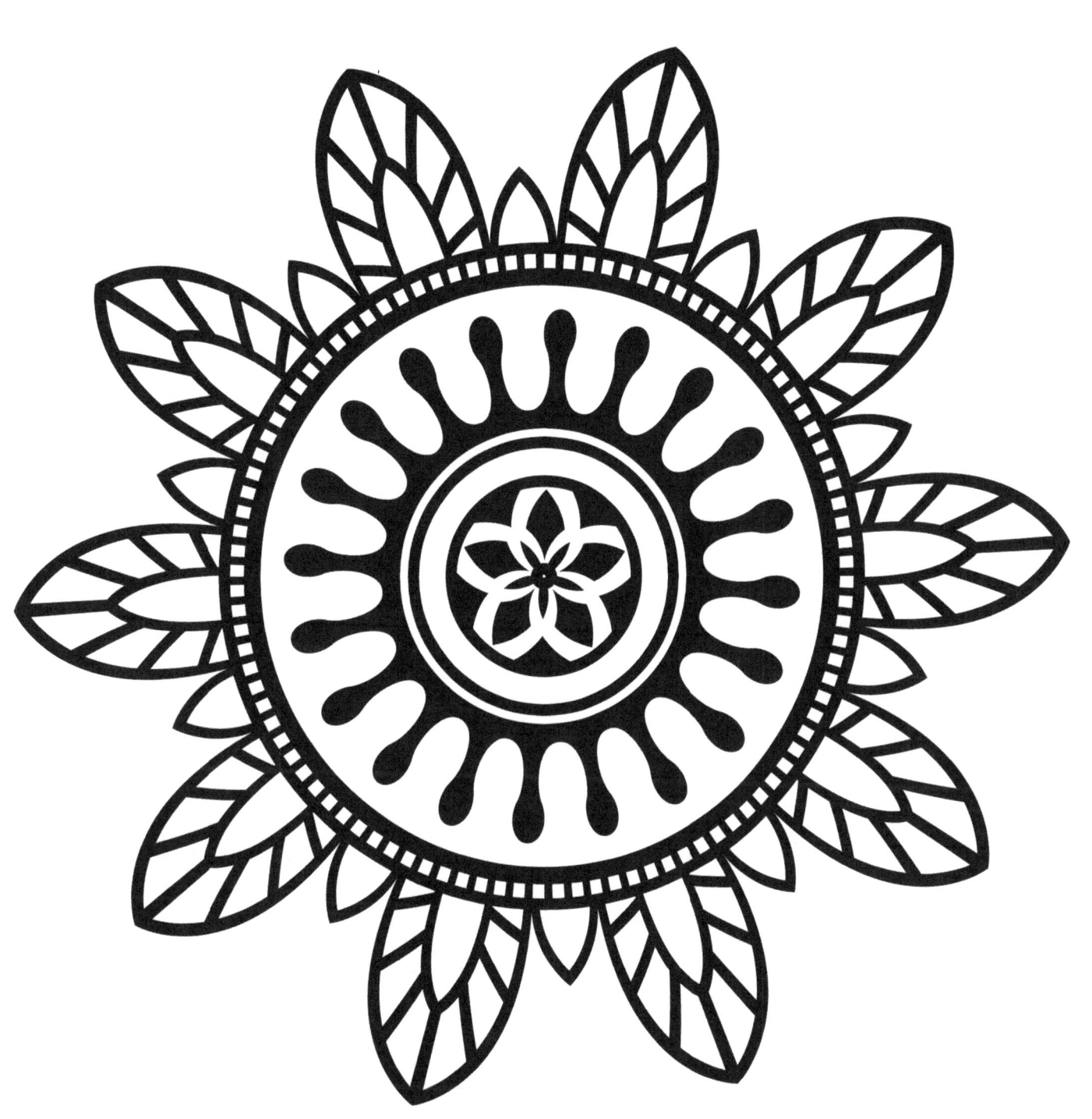

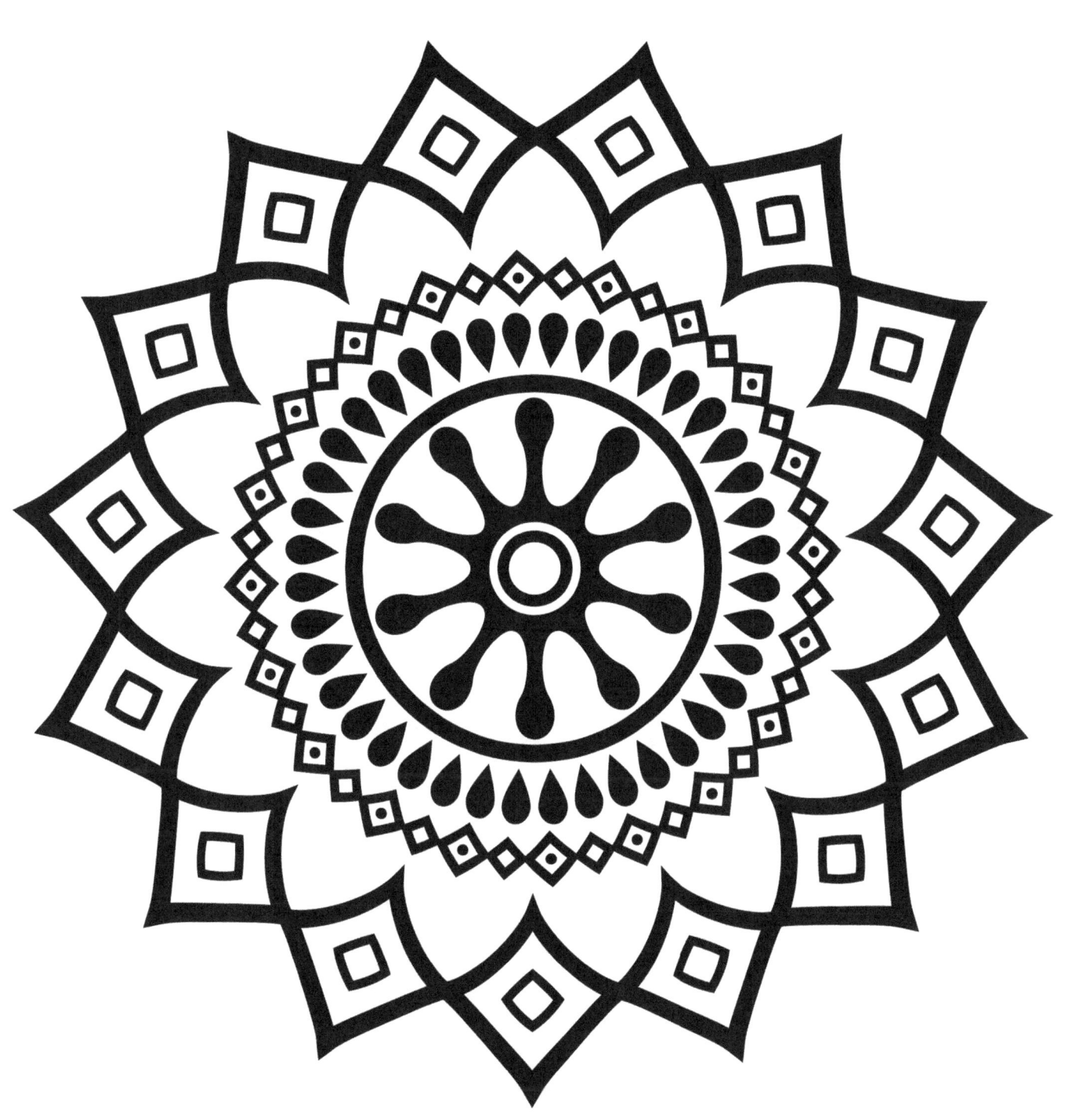

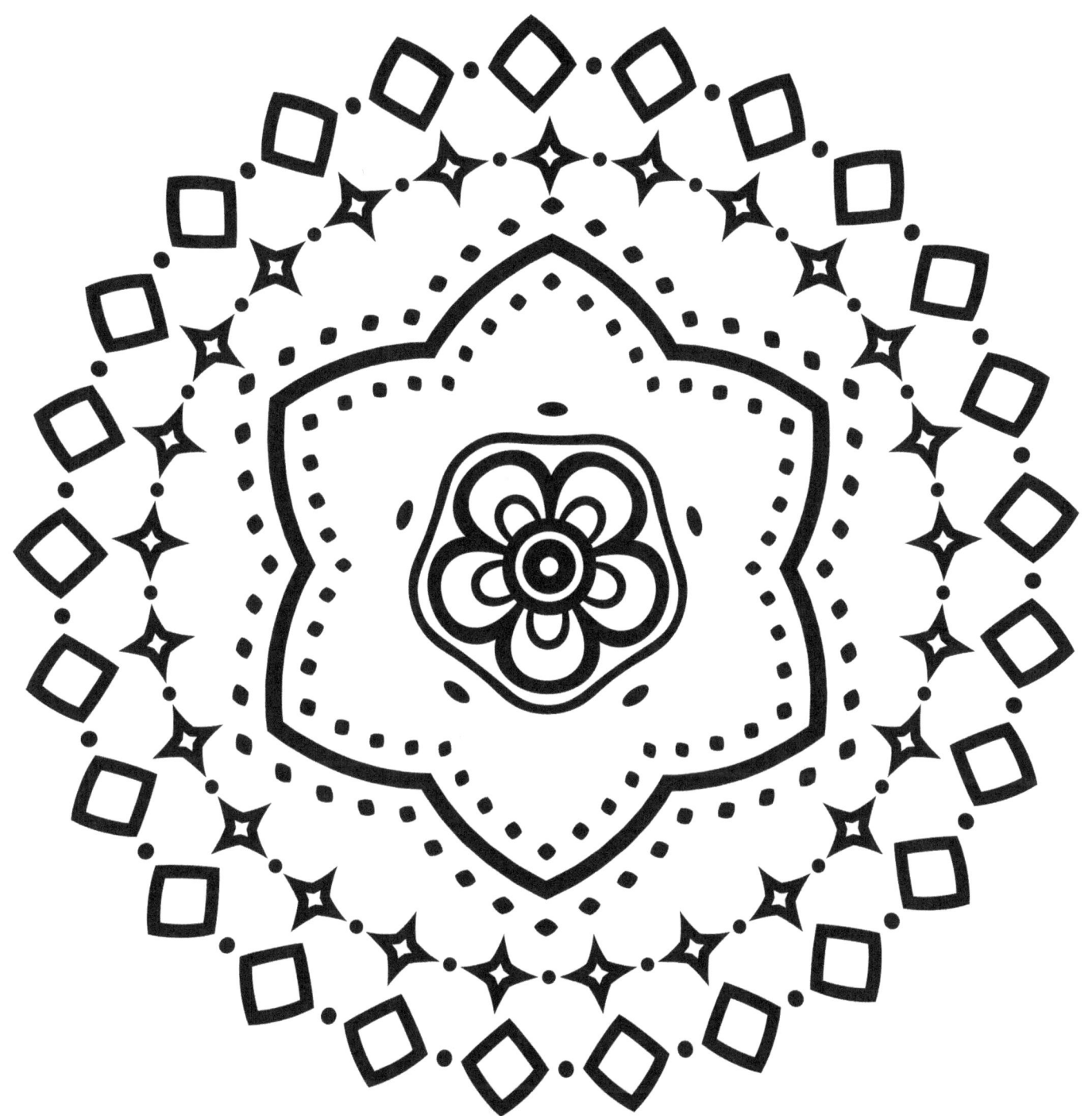

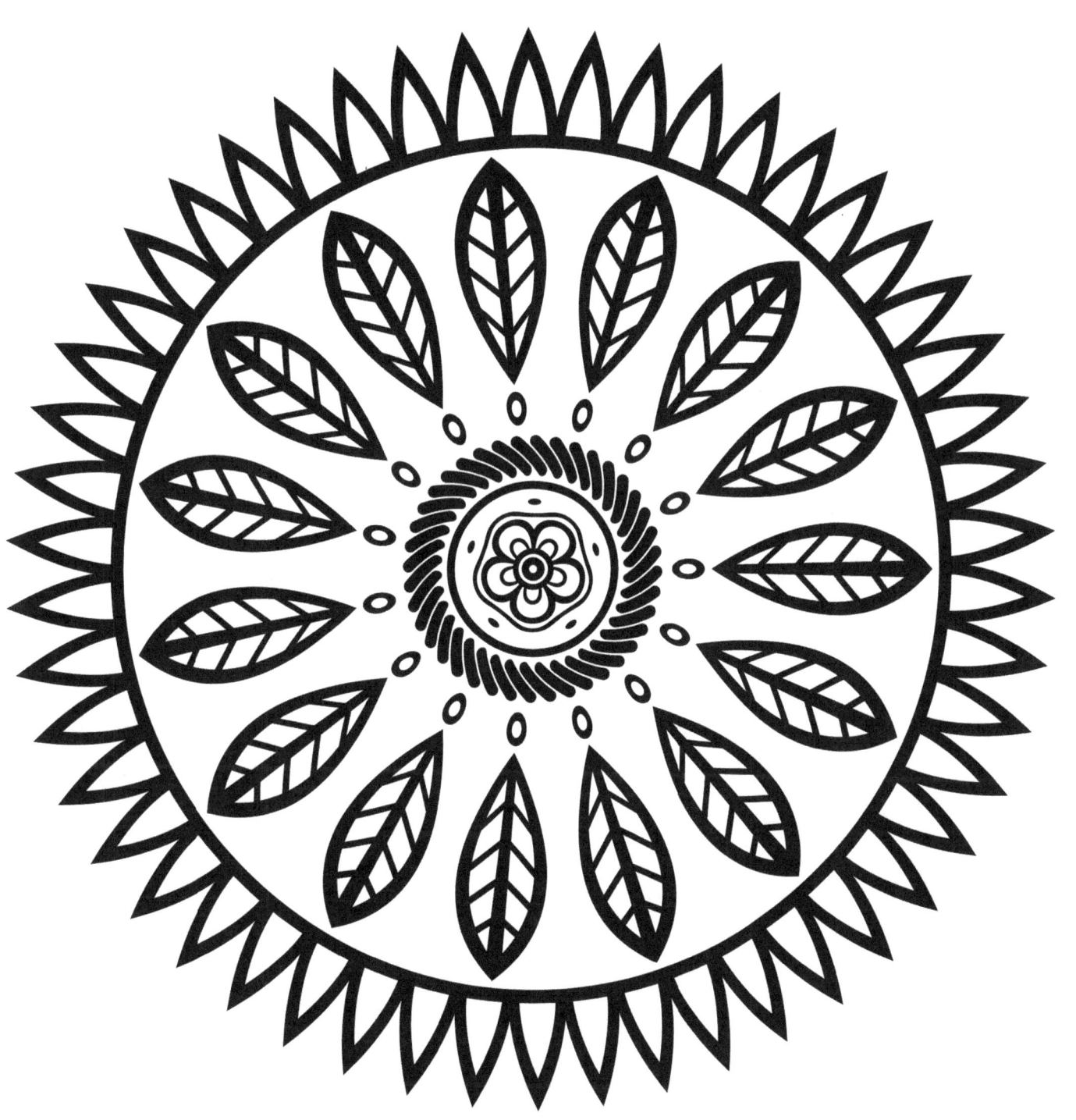

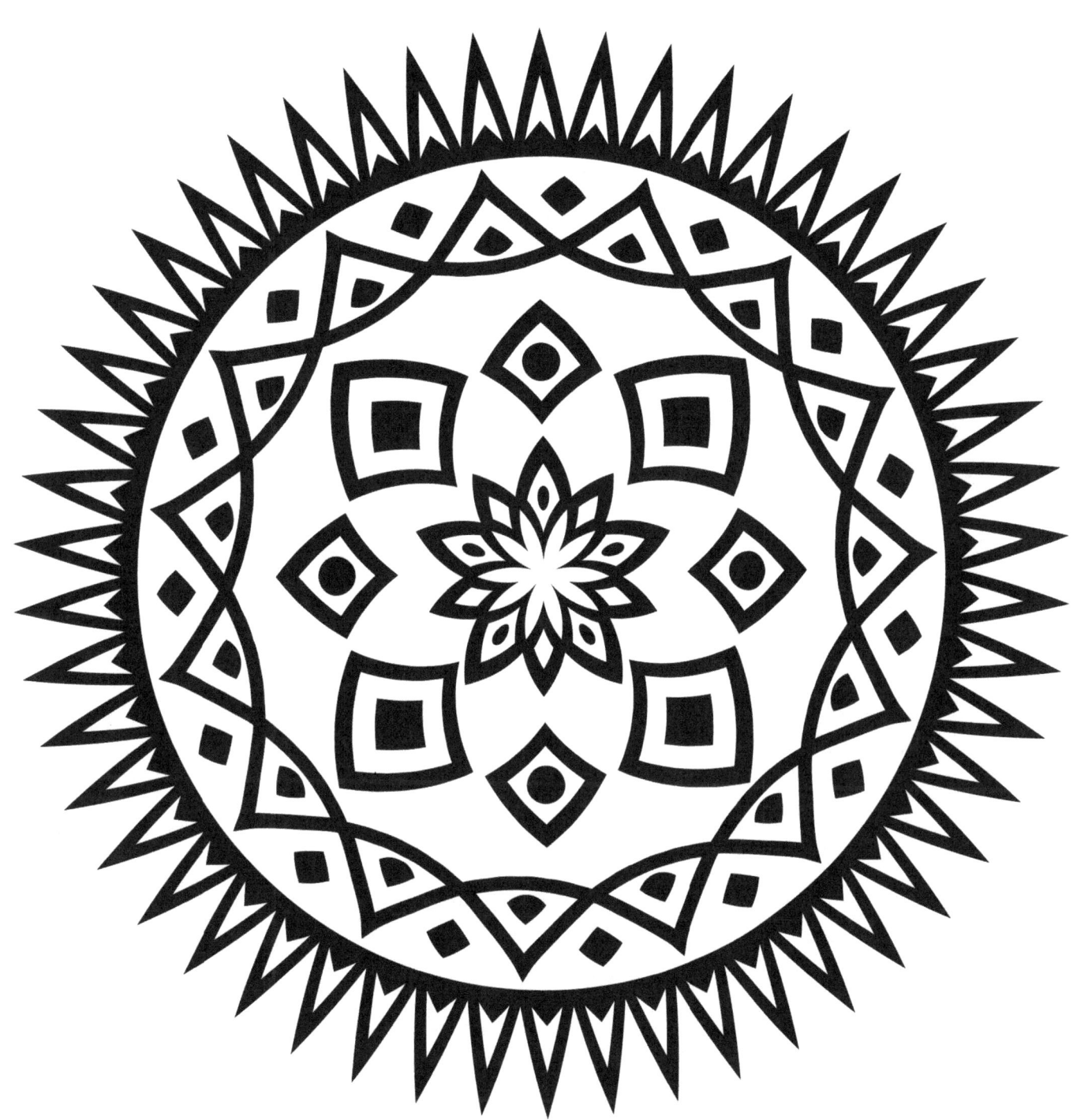

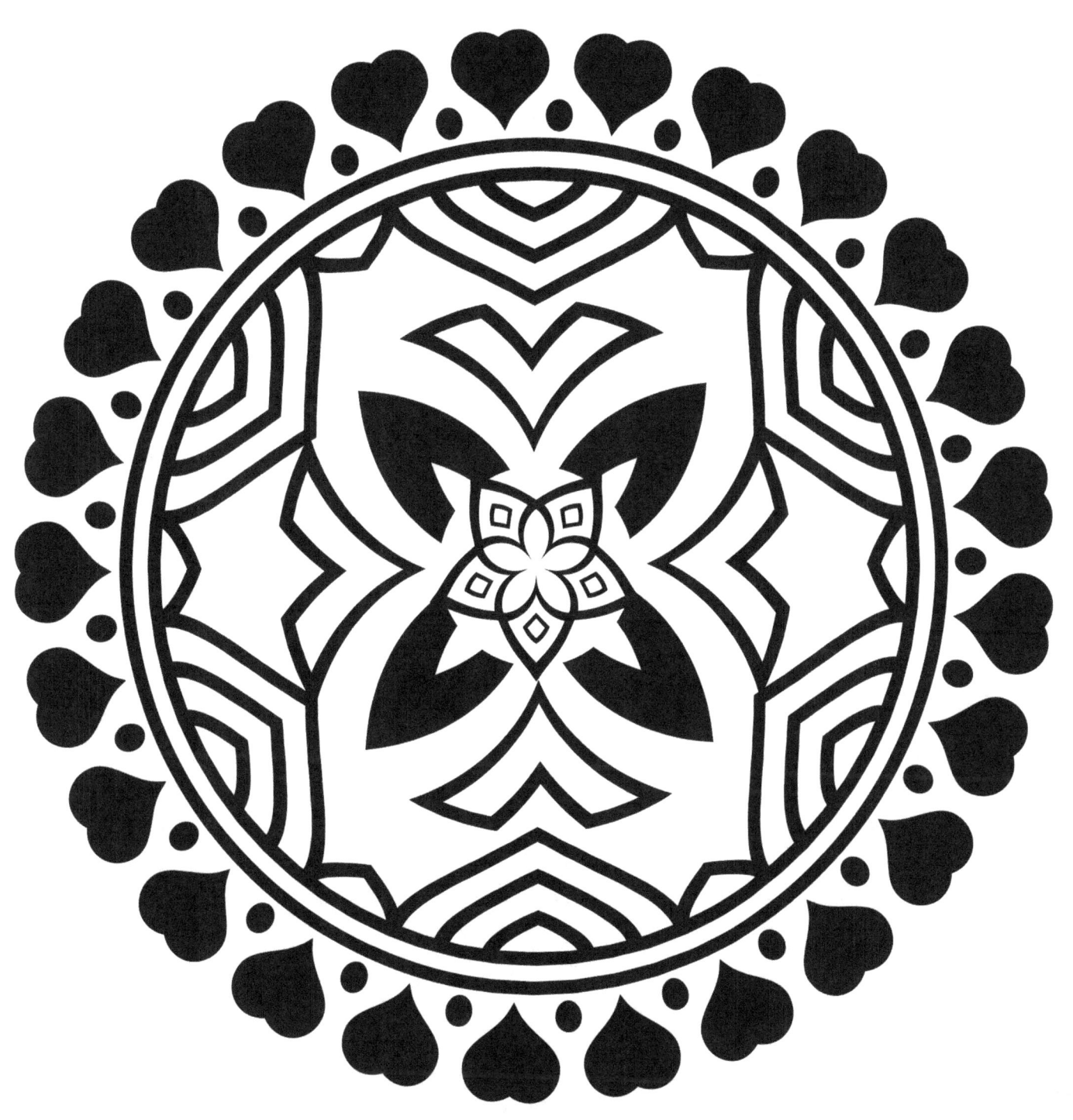

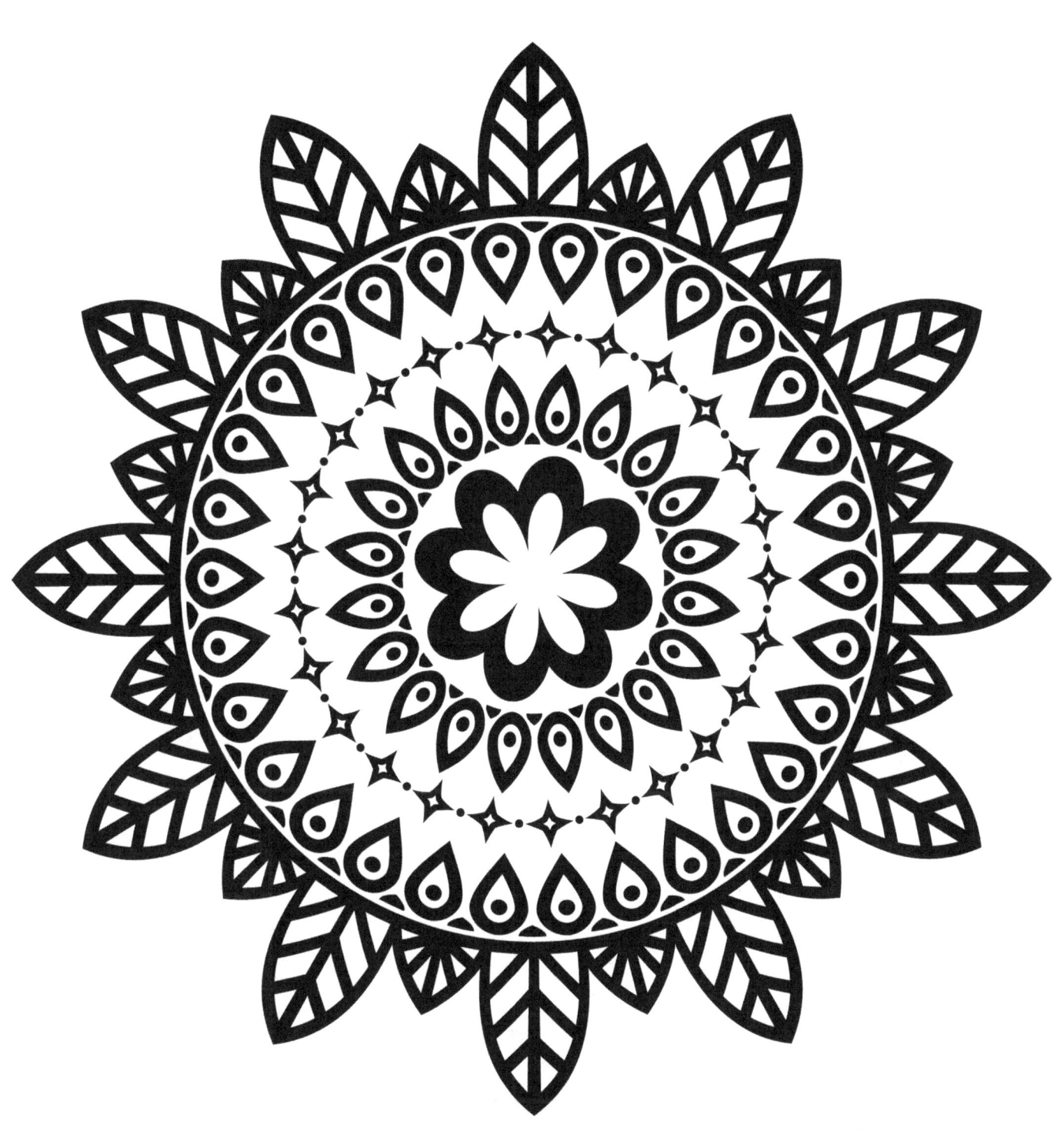

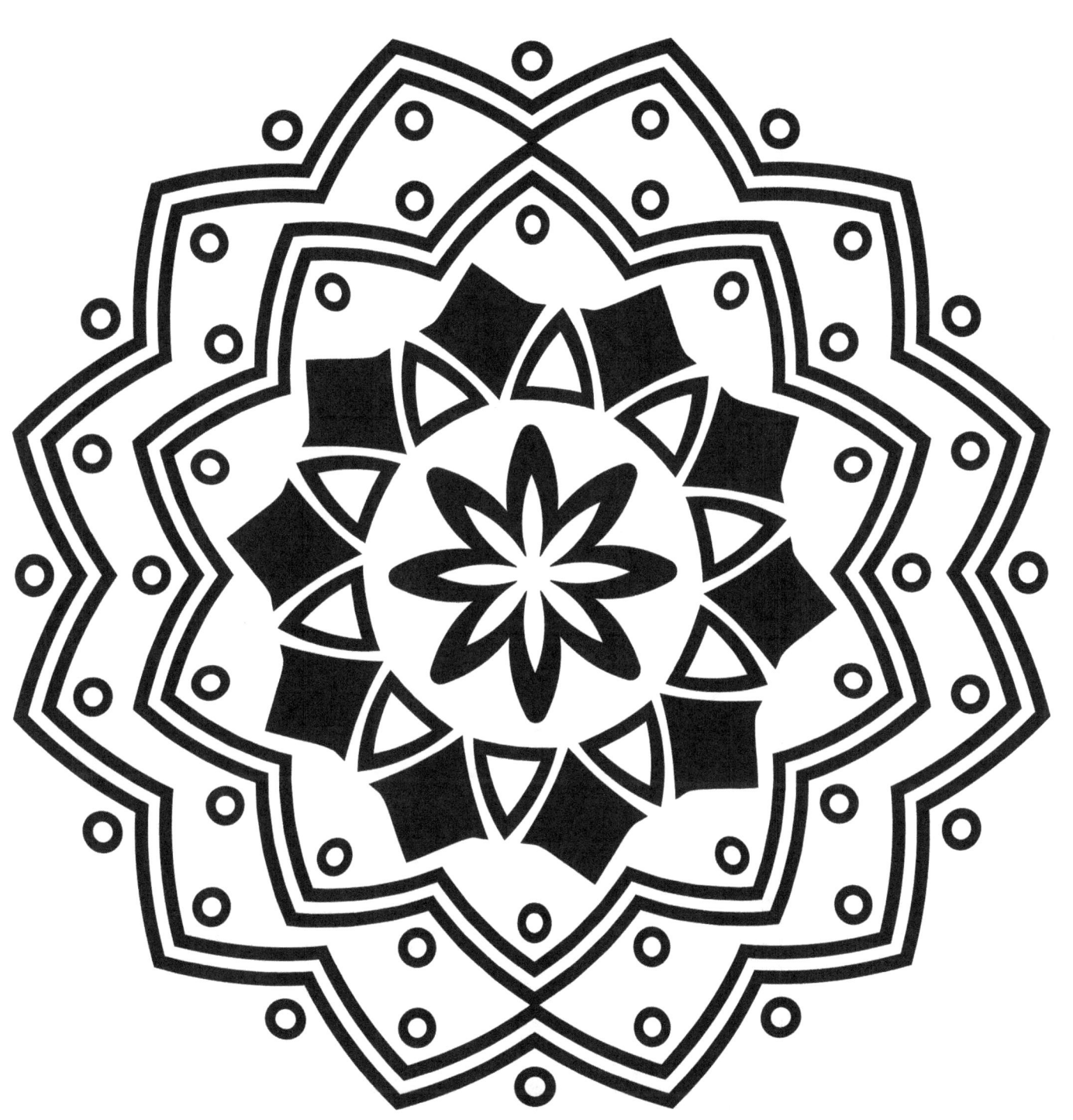

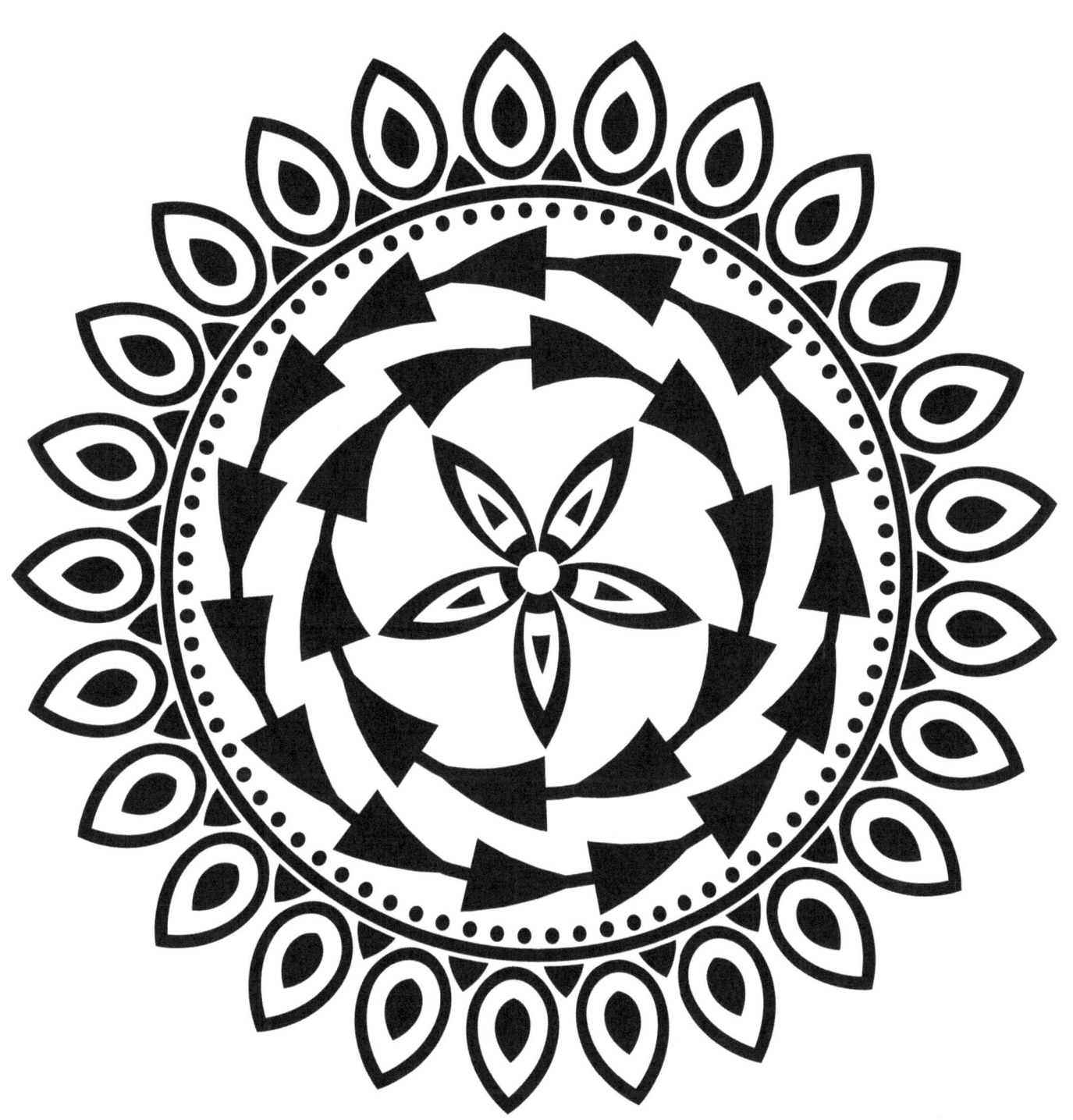

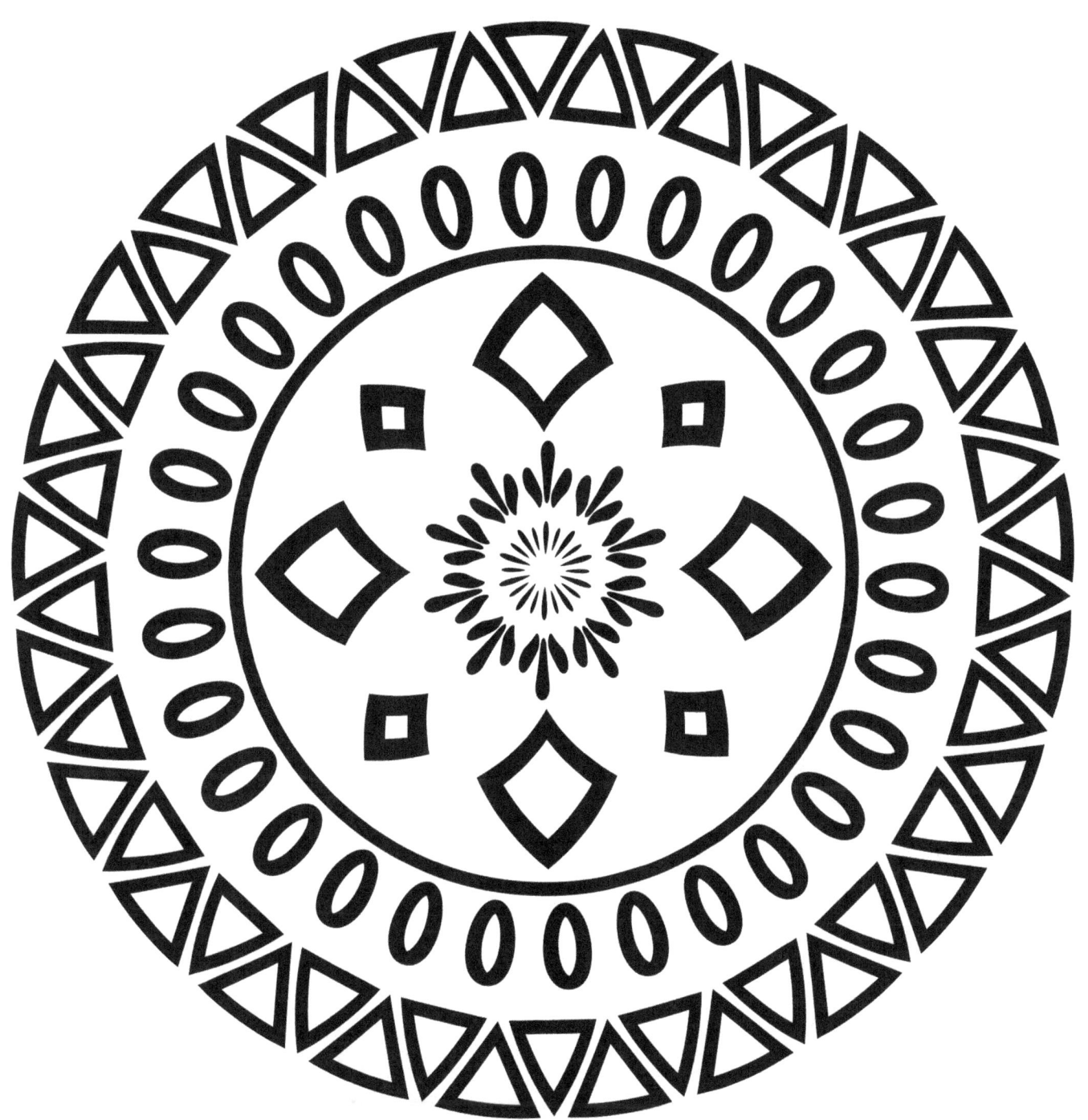

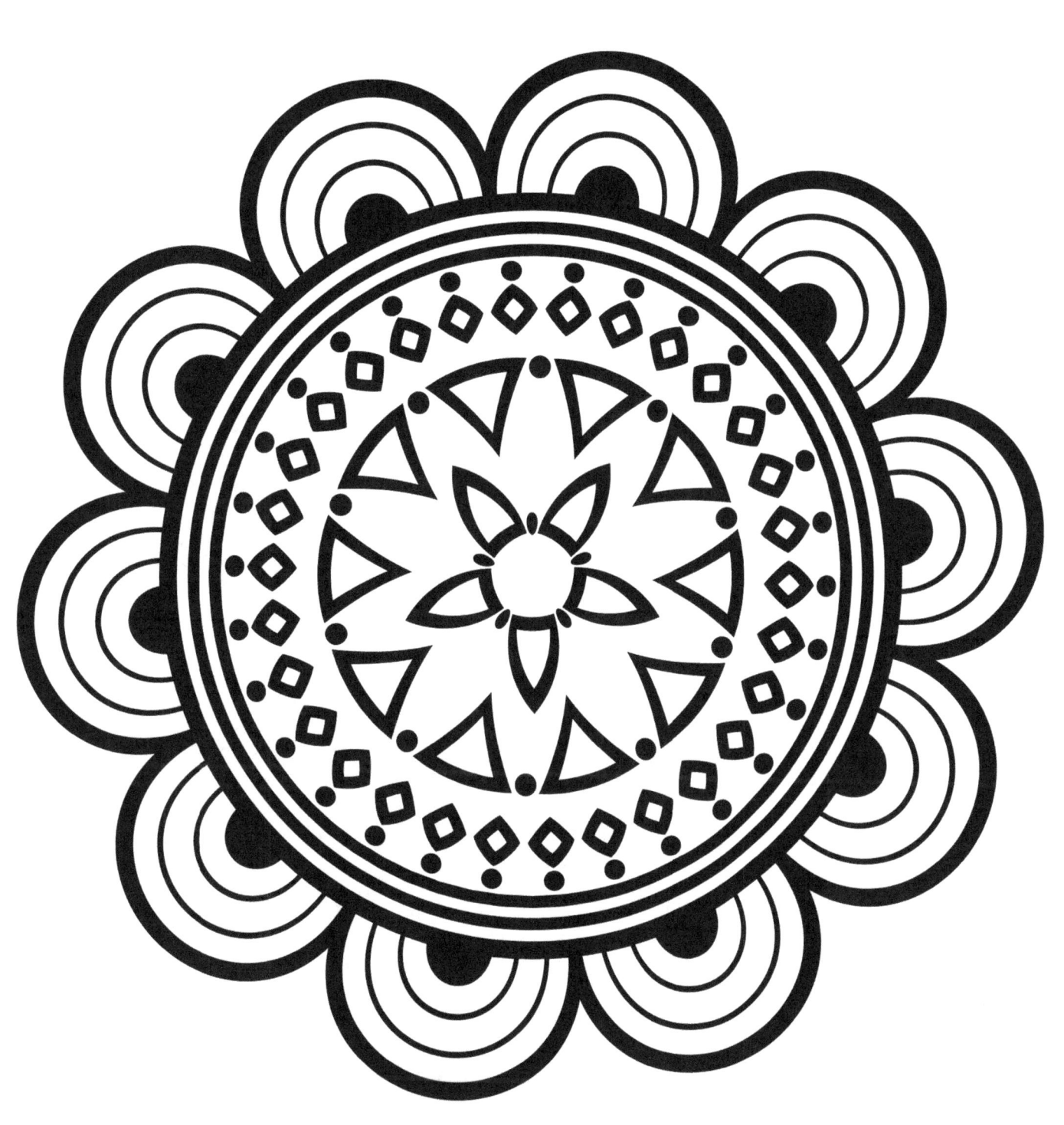

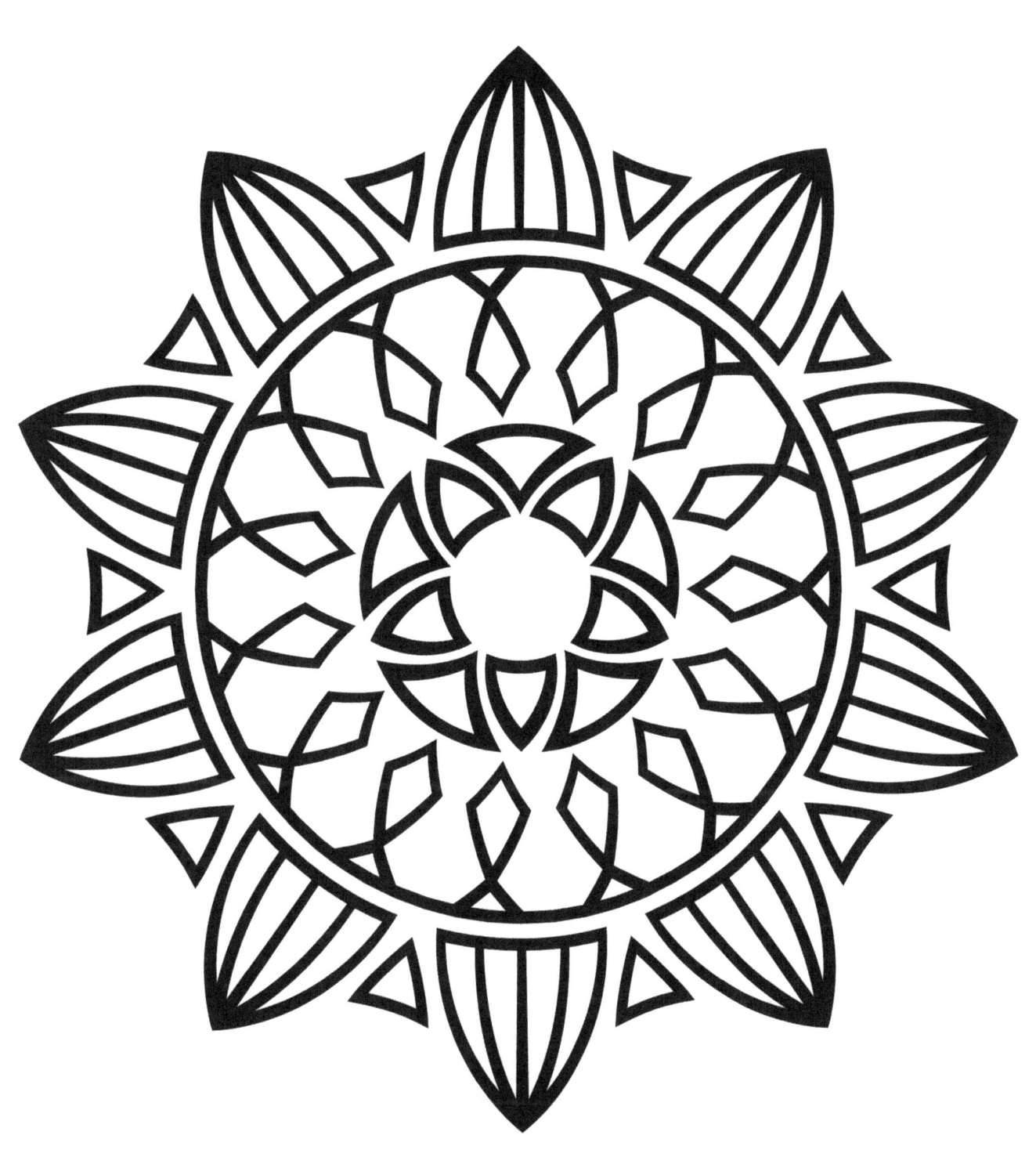

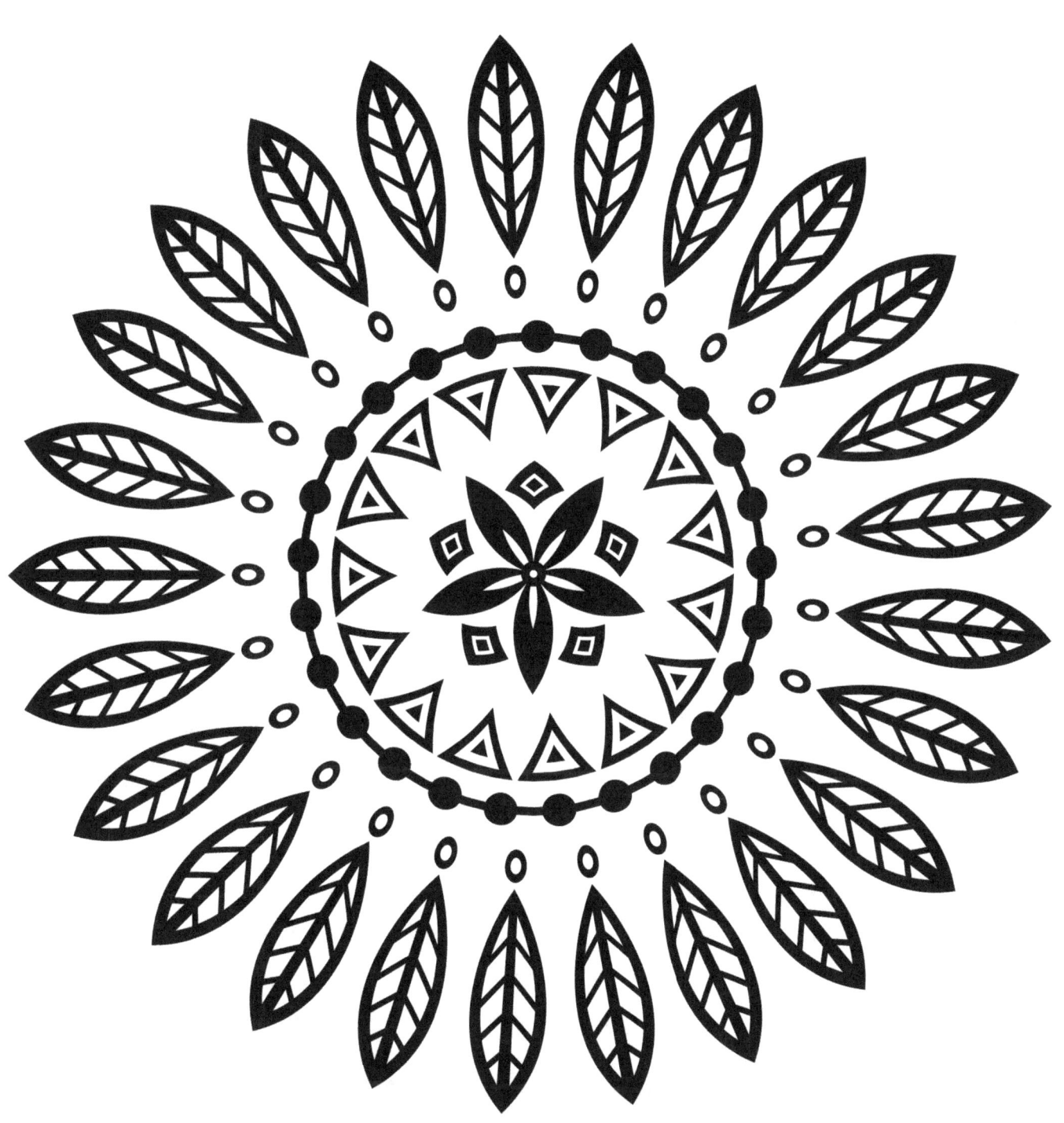

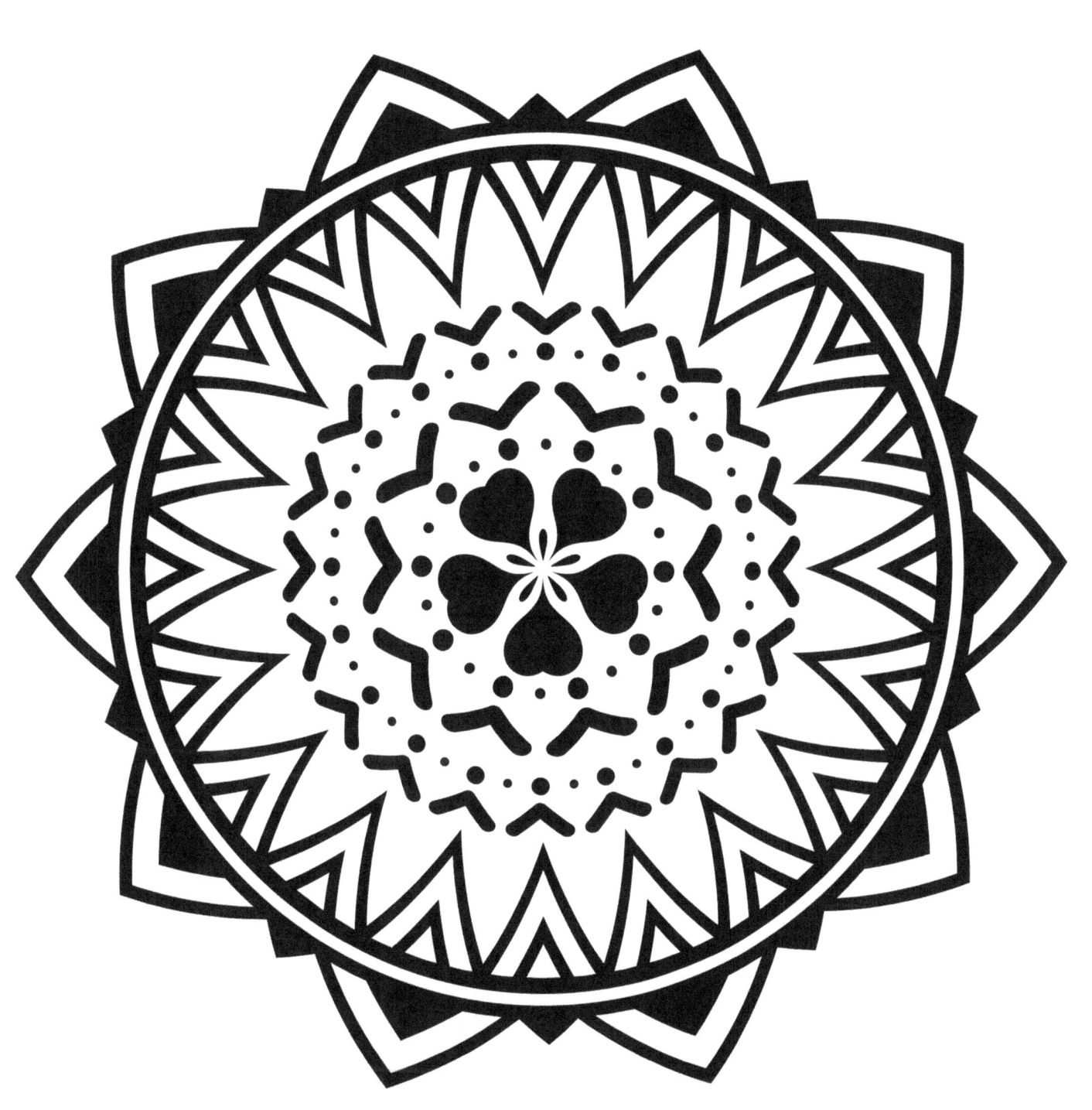

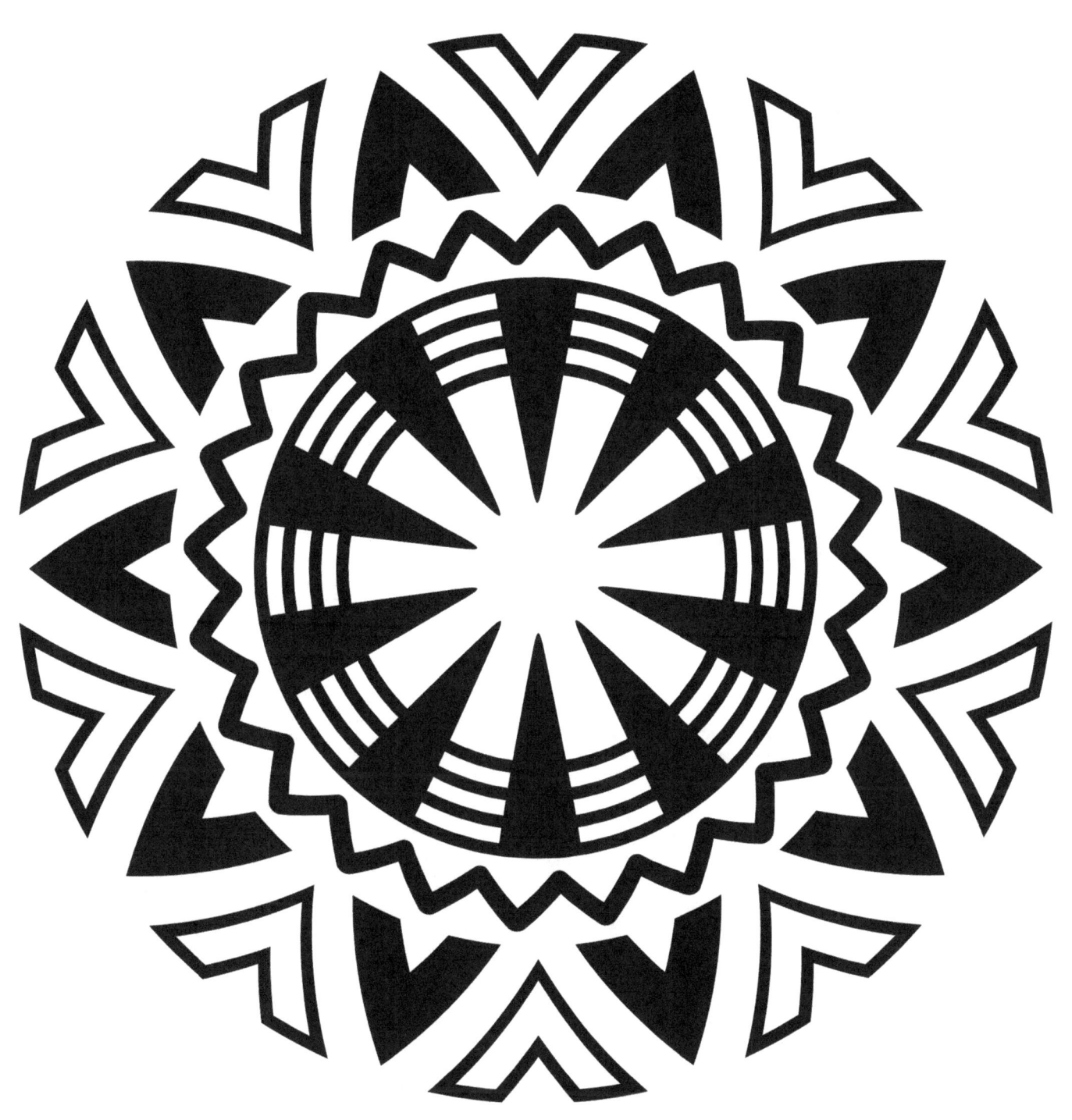

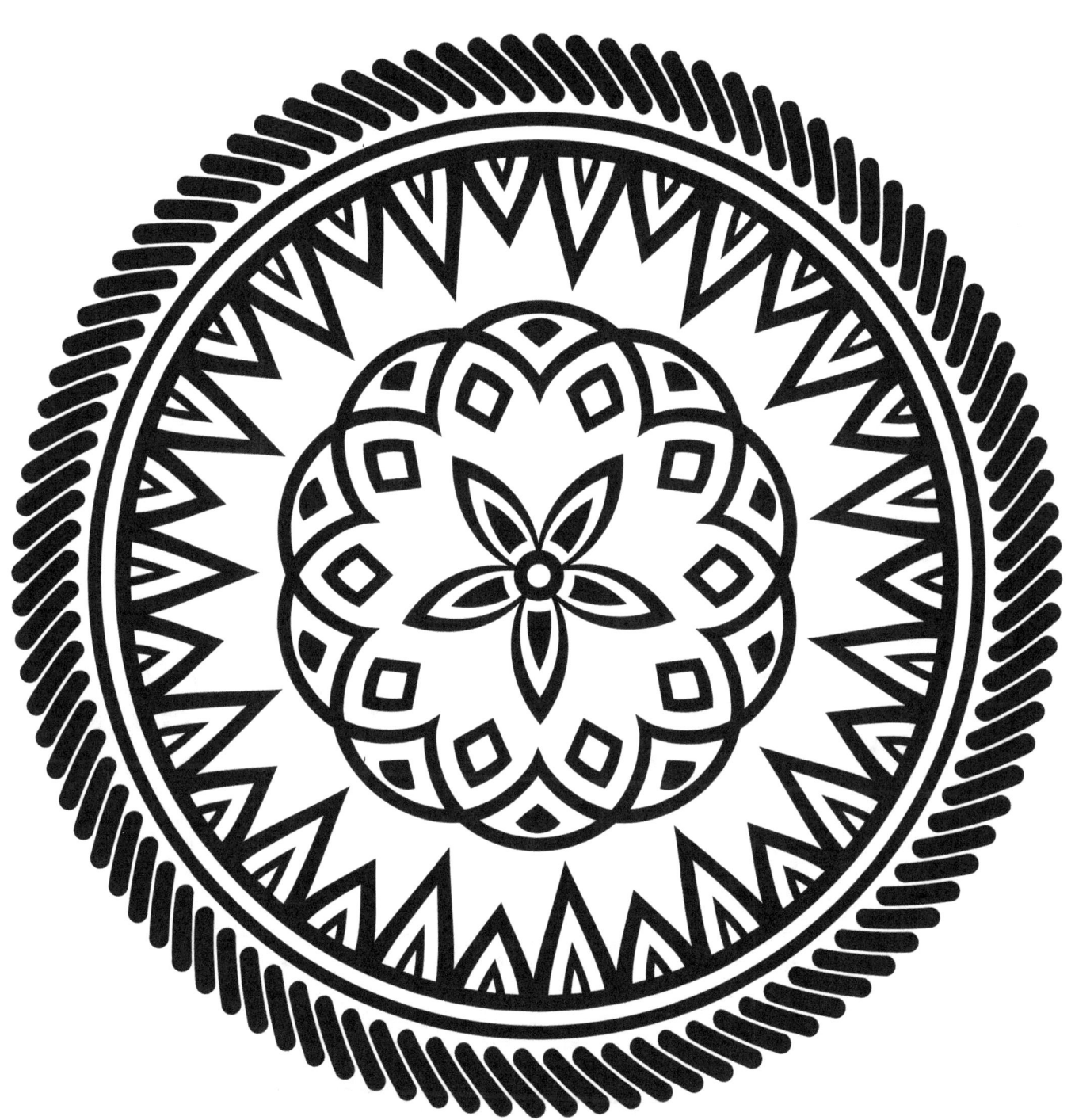

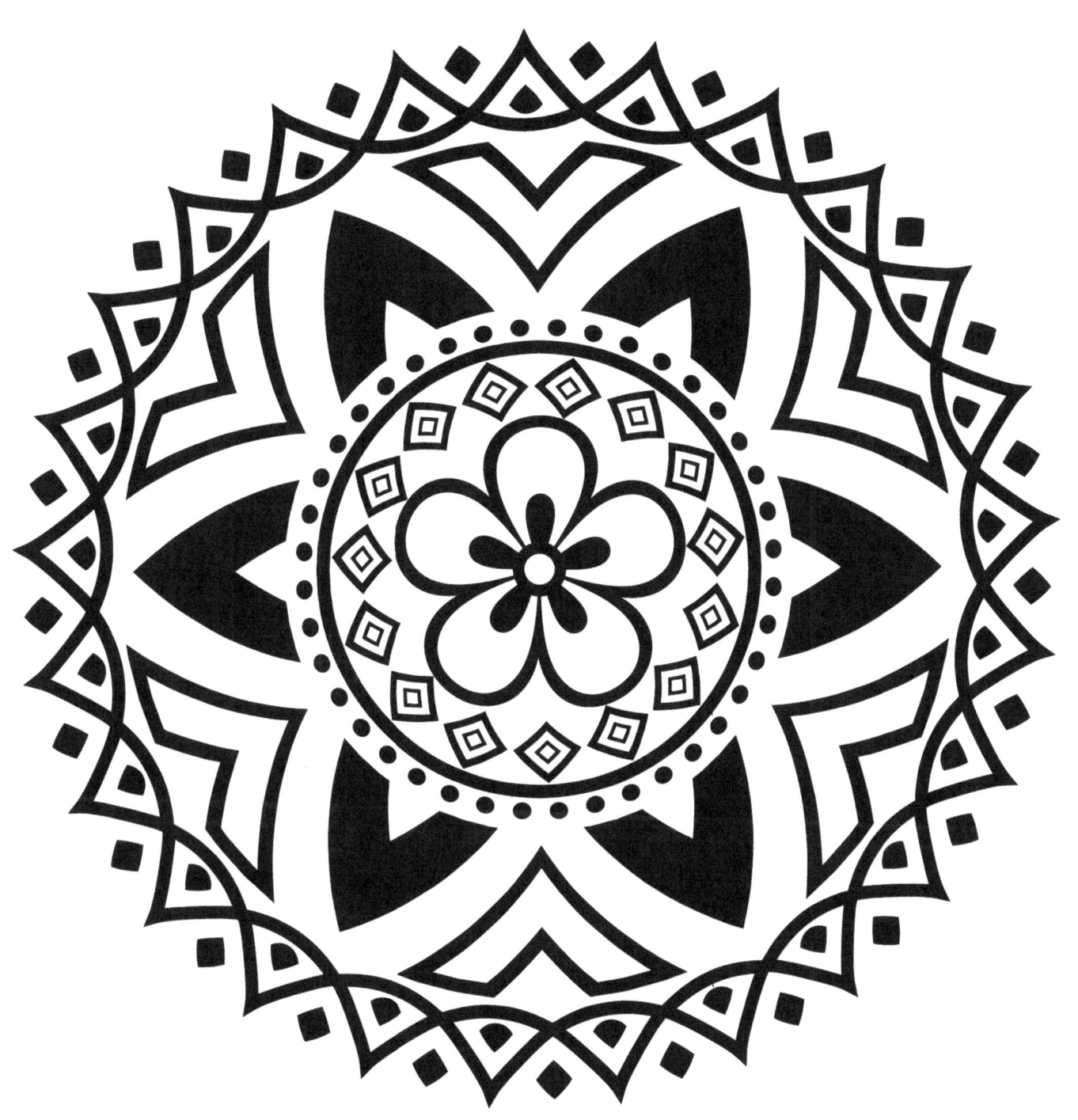

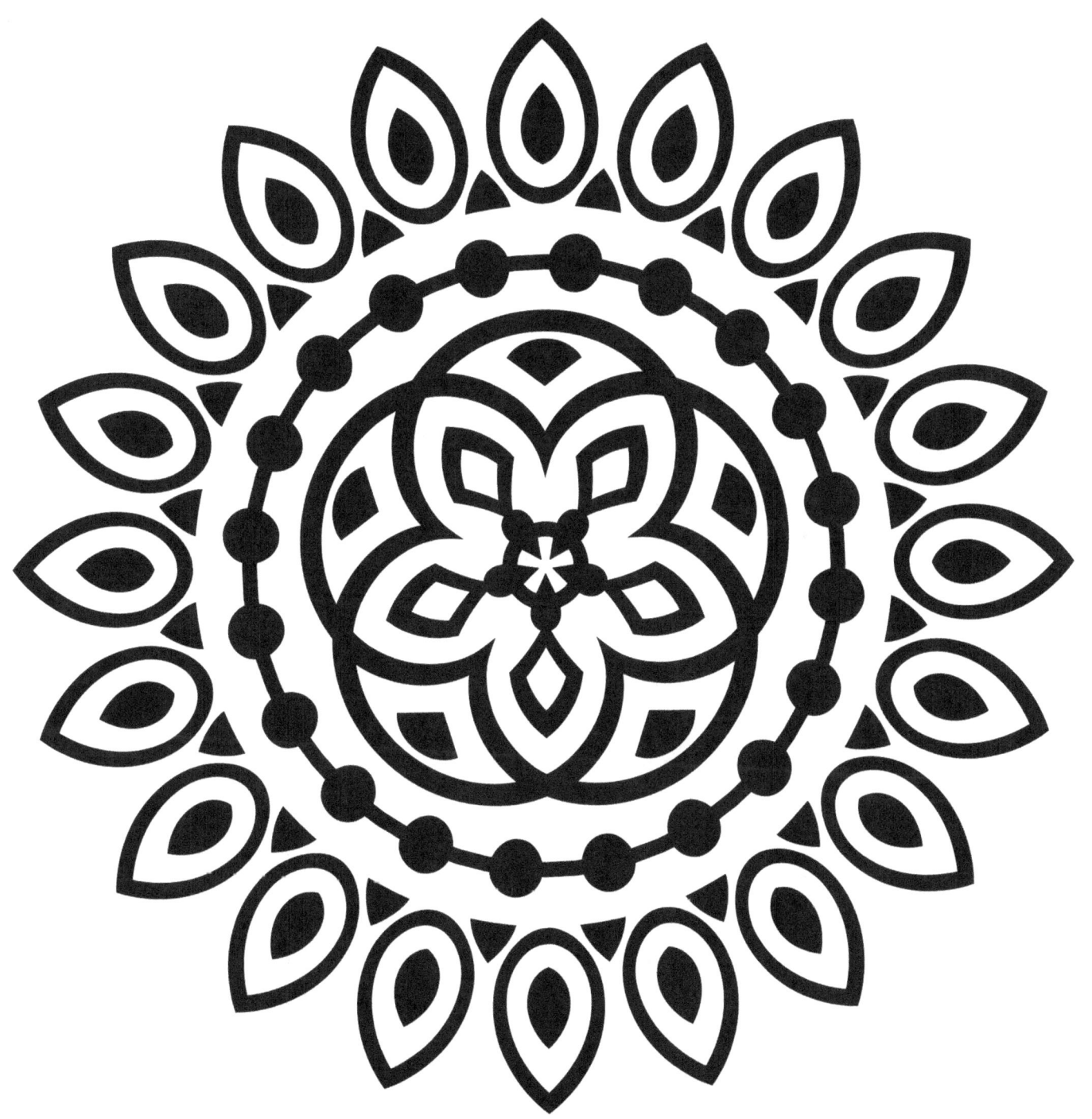